365

DAYS OF
PRAYER FOR

Depression
and Anxiety

BroadStreet
PUBLISHING

BroadStreet Publishing Group, LLC.
Savage, Minnesota, USA
Broadstreetpublishing.com

365 Days of Prayer for Depression & Anxiety
© 2020 by BroadStreet Publishing®

978-1-4245-6099-8 (faux leather)
978-1-4245-6100-1 (eBook)

Prayers composed by Sara Perry and Michelle Winger.

Design by Chris Garborg | garborgdesign.com
Editorial services by Michelle Winger | literallyprecise.com

Printed in China.

20 21 22 23 24 25 26   7 6 5 4 3 2 1

The LORD your God is living among you.
He is a mighty savior.
He will take delight in you with gladness.
With his love, he will calm all your fears.
He will rejoice over you with joyful songs.

ZEPHANIAH 3:17 NLT

Introduction

Whether you've read prayer books for many years or this is your first prayer devotional, inspiration is waiting for you in the daily prayers written here. The circumstances of life may have you feeling anxious, overwhelmed, discouraged, or even depressed. Isn't it encouraging to know that God's love is not dependent on your situation? Because his love for you is unchanging and his promises are true, you can choose to believe that today will be a good day.

Ultimately, prayer is a conversation with God. You don't need to use fancy words or recite long passages of Scripture. Just talk to God. Open your heart. He adores you, and he's listening.

Some days your prayers may be filled with gratitude, some days with repentance, and some with need. Just lay your prayers at the feet of God and wait for his powerful response. Rest in the compassion of your good Father. He listens to every word you utter, and he fully understands your heart.

As you develop a habit of prayer, think about this:

PRAISE

Begin by telling God how wonderful he is. Focus on which of his many attributes you are grateful for.

REPENTANCE

Before you present your needs to God, pause. Take a moment to examine your heart. If God reveals any unconfessed sin, bring it before him and ask for forgiveness.

ASK

What do you need from your Father in heaven today? Ask him boldly; he is waiting to grant you the desires of your heart.

YIELD

Ask as if it will be done and yield to his will. Acknowledge he may know something you don't or have something even better in mind for you. Trust and accept whatever answer you receive.

January

The earnest prayer
of a righteous person
has great power and produces
wonderful results.

JAMES 5:16 NLT

Never Alone

The LORD himself will go before you.
He will be with you;
he will not leave you or forget you.
Don't be afraid and don't worry.

DEUTERONOMY 31:8 NCV

God, nowhere in the Bible does it say that I should strive to do things on my own. Your Word repeatedly reminds me that you partner with the weak and willing and give them strength. You meet me where I feel the most vulnerable.

Thank you for being with me in the middle of my greatest triumphs and struggles. You have not forgotten about me. You pull me out of my confusion and angst. I choose to let go of my worry today and trust that you are at work in every single detail of my life.

Holy Spirit, I invite you into my weakness today. Give me eyes to see what you are doing as I cling to you. Thank you that I am not alone in any situation. Help me to remember today, above all else, that you are with me.

Unchanging One

Why are you in despair, O my soul?
And why have you become disturbed within me?
Hope in God, for I shall yet praise Him,
the help of my countenance and my God.

PSALM 42:11 NASB

God, I am not immune to feeling discouragement and despair. You are the lifter of my head and the source of all the help I need in every season. When anxiety fills my body and worries overshadow the goodness in my life, I turn to you, my good Father, because you never change.

When I feel overwhelmed, help me to take a moment to breathe and direct my soul's gaze to you because you see all and you are over all. Though I cannot control what will happen in this world, I can focus my heart on who you are, who you always have been, and who you will continue to be.

God, my help, fill me today with your Spirit. Breathe new life into my weary soul, causing hope to rise once again. I fix the eyes of my heart on your goodness and faithfulness for you never fail!

Delivered

Every time they cried out to you in their despair,
you were faithful to deliver them;
you didn't disappoint them.

PSALM 22:5 TPT

Father, you didn't promise me a pain-free life. No such thing exists! When I face trials and circumstances that oppose my hope and expectations, I come to you in desperation with everything I feel, including my fears, anxieties, and doubts.

There is no human experience that is outside of your understanding and no situation that is out of your reach. Help me to cry out to you in honesty. I don't want to hold back. I know that in your faithfulness you will not disappoint me.

Faithful One, I come to you with an open heart today. Let your light shine on the places I have kept hidden from you; I cry out from the depths of my soul for you to rescue me. Meet me in the middle of my mess, bringing order to the chaos. I trust you.

Steady

He lifted me out of the pit of despair,
out of the mud and the mire.
He set my feet on solid ground
and steadied me as I walked along.

PSALM 40:2 NLT

God, I feel like I am drowning under the weight of my circumstances. When darkness makes it hard to see where I'm going, please keep me from sinking into desperation. I was never meant to rely on my limited resources to get out of tough situations.

Where I feel stuck, I cry out to you for help. I invite you into the specific places that overwhelm me. I believe that you will lift me out of the muck and set my feet on solid ground. I know you can do it. You are faithful to meet me no matter what kind of mess I find myself in. You rescue me, your beloved child, over and over again.

Father God, I need your help. Show up in my life with your resurrection power, bringing life out of what has felt like death. Fill my heart with hope as I watch your faithfulness unfold before my very eyes.

Hopeful Heart

Anxiety weighs down the heart,
but a kind word cheers it up.

PROVERBS 12:25 NIV

When the worries of life weigh down my soul, God,
sometimes I try to soldier on and just get through the day.
It is exhausting to try to keep it together when anxiety is
coursing through my body though. You are full of kindness
and so much more gentle than I expect.

If I come to you with my burdens, you are faithful to take
the weight of them and help me. You never turn away; you
do not need to take time to consider whether it's worth it,
for your love knows no limits! I can never reach the end of
your incredible kindness. When it feels too good to be true,
I know I have stumbled into your goodness. You are always
better than I expect.

Kind Father, I so easily forget the nature of your goodness
especially toward me. Lift the weight of my anxious
thoughts and bring peace and clarity to my mind. Fill my
body with your love that casts out every fear. May my heart
once again know the joy of loving you.

Unbothered

They do not worry about how short life is,
because God keeps them busy
with what they love to do.

ECCLESIASTES 5:20 NCV

Father, in this day and age, it's so easy to get swept up
in the digital world and to pass time without considering
what I am filling it with. If I were intentional about doing
things I love, my life would look a lot different.

I have one short life to live on this earth. How I spend
my time reflects how I live. Whether intentionally or not,
the time passes. Help me to live with my eyes fixed on a
goal, so I don't just let time pass without engaging in my
purpose. You are masterful in your plans. When I yield my
life to you, you are faithful to direct me.

Lord, you hold all my days. You see the end from the
beginning and every space in between. I offer you my life
again. Restore meaning where I have felt aimless. Ease the
worries of my mind with your boundless grace. Your ways
are so much better than my own, and you know me better
than I know myself. Lead me, Lord.

Shielded

You, O LORD, are a shield about me,
my glory, and the lifter of my head.

PSALM 3:3 ESV

When storms of life rage, I find shelter in you. Your Word says that you are my help in times of trouble. I can rely on you to guard me and keep me secure. You shield me from the fiery darts of the enemy—the lies that distort my true identity as a child of the Most High.

When the chaos of life makes it hard to see what is up from down, you are a steady rock to stand upon. Your Word is unfailing, and all your promises come to pass. You are lifter of my head, my strong help. You hold onto me when I don't have the strength to reach out to you. I lift my eyes to your gaze today. Help me to see a loving Father who will never let me go.

God my strength, when I am worn down from the hits that life gives, I need you to hold me up. Be my defender; I can't fight these battles on my own. I don't even want to. You, Lord, are faithful and I trust you. Cover me with your love as I lean into your arms today.

Resilient

We are hard pressed on every side, but not crushed;
perplexed, but not in despair.

2 CORINTHIANS 4:8 NIV

God, when the storms of life are harsh and seem unending, I
have an opportunity to make a choice. I can either give into
despair or hold onto hope, which will cause me to persevere.
I can't do this on my own; rather, I rely on your Holy Spirit
who continually fills me with your love. It is this unrelenting
love that has the strength to overpower every fear.

When I feel overwhelmed and my thoughts are full of
worry, I choose to fix my eyes on you. I remember Jesus'
life of love that overcame death and destruction. My
inheritance is life!

Jesus, when I look at your life, I see the evidence of love
beyond my greatest imaginings. I set my gaze on you
today, remembering that you have overcome the world.
With your life in mine, I can overcome too.

Kingdom Bearer

He has delivered us from the power of darkness and conveyed us into the kingdom of the Son of His love.

COLOSSIANS 1:13 NKJV

God, you are the deliverer and protector. In you I find that I am both kept secure and freed to move. I have been brought from darkness into light, where everything is made clear. Where there seemed to be no way, you made a way for me to be restored. Your love never fails. It is the driving force of all creation, and what fuels the restoration work you are constantly doing.

I belong to a kingdom of love, full of compassion and mercy. There is plenty of room for me; those who struggle always have access to your strength through your grace. There is never a circumstance too difficult or a problem too great that you don't already have a solution for. As I look to you, I find that I bear your signature—I have been marked by love.

God over all, you are my deliverer. When I don't know where to turn and confusion threatens to immobilize me, you step in with your peace and your steady hand guides me. You are full of compassion at every point. Thank you for your deliverance. I depend on you still!

Sweet Words

Kind words are like honey—
sweet to the soul and healthy for the body.

PROVERBS 16:24 NLT

Father God, it is amazing how a kind word can crack the hard layer of my heart that is prone to protect itself. When sweet, genuine words are spoken, they build up my soul and encourage my heart. Proverbs says that they even bring health to my body.

When I consider my thought life and the words I speak over myself, I don't often reflect the kindness with which you speak over me. Sometimes it is easier to be kinder to others. Help me to treat myself with the same kindness I treat my loved ones. It is a good day to reconsider my worth.

Holy Spirit, I ask for your awareness today to know what it is that God thinks of me. In light of his great love, give me the grace to be kind to myself, as intentionally loving and patient as I would be with a child. I want to see myself through eyes of love the way you do.

Confidence

Faith is confidence in what we hope for
and assurance about what we do not see.

HEBREWS 11:1 NIV

God, there is so much changing in my life on a regular basis. It is difficult to know what I can cling to in a world that is always shifting. When it comes down to it, what are the unshakeable tenets of my faith? God, in your love, you make it clear that you are unchanging.

My understanding of your goodness may fluctuate, sometimes multiple times a day, but your character remains constant. My confidence lies in you. I don't want to rely on my own intelligence, strength, or determination to succeed in life. When all else fails, I only have you to hold onto. I open my heart to your Spirit of wisdom.

Unchanging One, you are the only constant in a continuously changing world. I ask for your perspective on my life today; I want to see things from your point of view. Let my confidence be in you, not found in something that will inevitably shift. All my hope is in you.

Freedom

We have freedom now,
because Christ made us free.
So stand strong.
Do not change and go back
into the slavery of the law.

GALATIANS 5:1 NCV

Jesus, the beautiful reality of the Gospel is that you sacrificed your life so I would be free from the chains of sin and death. You paved a way to the Father so nothing would keep me from you again. No hardship, no struggle, no addiction, nothing can keep me from your great love. I want to live in the reality of this great freedom.

I have the choice to live unbound, nothing holding me back from your persistent grace. I have been welcomed into your family as a dearly loved child. I am not a weird, estranged cousin. I am yours. I belong to you. No wall, no chains, no fear, and no doubt can keep me from you.

God, your relentless grace has covered my life and set me free to choose my way. My past does not dictate my future, nor do my struggles get to direct my life. I align myself with you and your kingdom today. May your freedom reign in my life, opening up what was once restricted.

Filled

From his fullness we have all received,
grace upon grace.

JOHN 1:16 NRSV

Father, in the whirlwind of life, it is so easy to feel depleted. There is always more to do, further needs to be met and seemingly endless demands on my attention and time. I was never intended to live in a constant state of lack. You have everything I could ever need. You are full of grace for every moment of my life.

My brokenness is not too much for you, and my weakness does not disturb you. In your heart of love, there is everything I need for healing. You have already made accessible to me every tool I need to succeed, for you are the source of all life. I want to come to you and be filled.

God of abundance, in you is all I am longing for and everything I need. Fill me up with your grace that empowers me to live connected to you. I need you more than I know how to express. Meet me with your unfailing love today.

Unseen

We don't focus our attention on what is seen
but on what is unseen.
For what is seen is temporary,
but the unseen realm is eternal.

2 Corinthians 4:18 tpt

God, what I focus my attention on matters. Your kingdom is full of the treasures found in your unfailing love. When I spend my time caught up in the changing circumstances of my life without grounding myself in the reality of eternity, it can be overwhelming.

When I shift my awareness to your character, I am looking with eyes that see the promise of your kingdom to come because you are faithful to do all you said you would. Help me to fix my eyes on you, the author and perfecter of my faith. You never waver in kindness, and your compassion never ends. When I look for evidence of your goodness, I will surely find it.

Lord, help me to fix my eyes on you and on eternity rather than on the momentary troubles around me. Give me your perspective, so I may see the way you do. Fill my thoughts with yours, Lord, and make me more like you.

Rest

"Come to me,
all you who are weary and burdened,
and I will give you rest."

MATTHEW 11:28 NIV

God, when I find myself overextended and exhausted, the worries of life spill over from one day to the next, adding layer upon layer until I feel like I can't take another step. You invite me to come to you and lay down my heavy burdens. You are able to give me the rest that I long for as you do all the heavy lifting.

I don't want to hesitate to approach you with all I have; you are waiting with open arms. You are full of kindness not a lecture that I dread. Your gentleness surprises me as I offer you my heaviness. You fill me with light and life! Help me to find rest in you today.

Kind Father, I come to you today with all the heaviness I've been carrying. I can't keep going on this way. Lift my burdens and fill me with the peace that gives true rest to my soul. I need you.

Strength for Today

My life's strength melts away with grief and sadness;
come strengthen me and encourage me with your words.

PSALM 119:28 TPT

God, sometimes the stresses of life, even the small,
mundane, and ordinary things, feel like too much to face.
I find myself relying on my own motivation to get through
the days or weeks. Other times I feel like sadness has
stripped away any desire to do anything outside of the
necessary.

Father, you are faithful to give me strength in my every
weakness. There is not a day where I am left on my own
to figure things out. Your grace is always available to
empower and strengthen me, though that may not look
like getting done everything I'd hoped. Your strength
carries me. When I am stripped of the enthusiasm I once
had for life, I want to adjust my expectations of what
strength looks like. I want your personal and profound
encouragement today.

Holy One, you are the strength that carries me through
my darkest days. I won't worry about what tomorrow will
bring; today, I fix my eyes on you. Come strengthen and
encourage me like only you can.

Hopeful Expectation

The helpless has hope,
and unrighteousness must shut its mouth.

JOB 5:16 NASB

As a child is completely dependent on their parents to provide what they cannot, so am I dependent on you, Father God. When I find myself out of my depth and overcome with helplessness, I want to turn to you. There are some circumstances that can't be fixed by anything I could even dream of offering.

If my hope is in my own strength and capabilities, I will fail. I want my hope to lie in the one who formed me and everything around me. Your character is flawless and your faithfulness is unmatched. This limited life is not where the fulfillment of my expectation will be found, though I have sweet glimpses of my eternal hope. There is coming a day where there will be no more tears or sadness, and the old will have passed away. Help my confidence to lie in you.

God over all, you are bigger than I can fathom. I'm so grateful that you see from a higher perspective than I do. I ask for your holy hope to fill my heart today with the confidence of your goodness. You are worthy!

Wait

For God alone, O my soul, wait in silence,
for my hope is from him.

PSALM 62:5 ESV

Sometimes waiting feels like sitting in a fluorescent-lit office, anticipating my name being called, God. Other times, it is more like fighting a battle, awaiting reinforcements to come refuel my waning resources and turn the tide of the war. In my waiting today, I anticipate your response.

There is so much strength and hope to be found in you, no matter how long my wait ends up being. Help me to yield my heart to you today, giving you space to speak your words of life over me. You delight over me with songs of deliverance; I will not be disappointed in the way you redeem my life!

God, I wait for you. When everything feels endless and barren, draw near and fill me with the fruit of your presence that never dissatisfies. You are so good; I cling to that reminder today. I quiet my heart before you now. Come and speak to me again.

Enough

"That is why I tell you not to worry about everyday life—whether you have enough food to eat or enough clothes to wear."

LUKE 12:22 NLT

God, when I take inventory of the worries that fill my mind, so many are based on what could happen in the future. My worries are often caught up in what-ifs and scenarios that may or may not ever happen. It seems like such a waste of time.

Jesus, when you spoke to your disciples, you said not to worry about everyday life. I will have what I need when I need it. There is always enough. I don't want my worries to drain my energy. I trust you to provide for everything I need. You are always on time. When I think through my life, there has never been a time when you left my needs unmet. Thank you for your faithfulness.

I can see how you have provided for me before, and I believe that you will do it again. I trust that you are sufficient for me and that you're never late. Fill my thoughts with your goodness.

Cast off Troubles

Banish anxiety from your heart
and cast off the troubles of your body,
for youth and vigor are meaningless.

ECCLESIASTES 11:10 NIV

God, there is no way to avoid troubles in this life. They come as surely as the seasons change. Anxieties mount as I consider how ill-equipped I am to face the challenges. My body reacts to the uncertainties I face. But this is not where my story ends. I am not destined to cycles of uncontrollable angst. You created my body, mind, and soul to be full of the peace that you freely give.

I want to feel your presence calm my anxious thoughts and bring peace to my hurried mind. Your Spirit gives comfort and fills me with your unfailing love that pushes fear aside. When I am worried, I ask you to draw near to me. You are faithful to come.

Holy Spirit, come fill me with the power of your presence. Bring peace to my anxious heart and calm my hurried mind. I rely on you. I cannot do it on my own, and I'm so glad that I don't have to. You are welcome to have your way in me, Lord, for I belong to you.

Goodness

I would have despaired unless I had believed
that I would see the goodness of the Lord
in the land of the living.

PSALM 27:13 NASB

I have such a great hope in what awaits me after this short life, God. And yet, it doesn't feel like enough to only hope for what feels so incredibly intangible. I need to know goodness in this life. Father, you are in the business of restoration. You deal in mending the wounded, binding up the brokenhearted, and bringing life out of dead things. You never give up or throw your hands up declaring something out of your reach.

When it feels like the end to me, I can rest in your promises that it is not. You always have a better plan. Plot twists may come, but your faithfulness never wavers. When disappointment is in my heart, there is also an invitation for your powerful presence to shift my perspective.

Good Father, I admit that I have felt the desperation of hard circumstances in my life. I have to believe that I will see your goodness again! Give me eyes to see that you are moving, even now, and tenacity to hold onto hope when it is difficult to decipher what you are doing.

Confident Help

We can say with confidence,
"The LORD is my helper, so I will have no fear.
What can mere people do to me?"

HEBREWS 13:6 NLT

Father, there are many situations that are completely out of my control. I cannot dictate the outcomes, and it sometimes seems that whatever I try to do to help only intensifies the issues. Tell me what to do, God. I don't need to be in control to be at peace. You are my help in every single circumstance.

You cannot be confused or confounded. My troubles are not too complex for you to handle. In your perfect wisdom, you always know exactly what to do. I just need to trust you to do what I can't. I relent my need to fix and ask you to be my help. You are more than capable in this, and every, situation.

Lord, you are my willing help in every hour of need. You never withdraw your presence, leaving me to figure things out on my own. I surrender my need to control and let you take the reins. You are always faithful. My confidence lies in you.

Humble Heart

God gives us even more grace,
as the Scripture says,
"God is against the proud,
but he gives grace to the humble."

JAMES 4:6 NCV

Failure is not a sin but an eventuality of humanity, God. It's ok to try and not succeed; it is not a character flaw to be imperfect. And when I do make mistakes that affect both myself and others in hurtful ways, there is so much grace. Not just enough grace but plentiful mercy that overflows!

When I humbly approach you, there is unfailing love that meets me every time. You don't sometimes encounter me with kindness and other times with harsh discipline. Even your correction is drenched in compassion. Let me not lose heart in approaching you at every opportunity. Your tender heart is full of power to heal, refine, and liberate.

God, I come to you with a humble heart, longing for your tender mercy to meet me again. I cannot test the limits of your compassion. There are no boundaries to your love. I offer myself as your own again; fill me with the power of your presence that sets me free.

Joy for Mourning

Those who sow in tears
shall reap with shouts of joy.

PSALM 126:5 ESV

When I am overcome by sadness, Comforter, you are close. There is no escaping pain in this life; it finds everyone in time. Broken promises, the loss of loved ones, and dashed hopes are all situations that I face. Even so, you are not surprised, and you are not distant.

Jesus, you were acquainted with suffering and familiar with pain. You did not require your followers to deny the reality of their circumstances; rather, you offered them hope in healing, joy in restoration, and the incredible satisfaction of right relationship with the Father. Whatever sorrows I am facing now will pale in comparison to the joy that is coming!

Lord, I cannot deny the sadness of my heart in heartbreak and in despair. In your goodness, touch me with the liquid love of your presence. Comfort me and revive my weary heart. There is no one who can do it, but I know that you can. Give me perspective to see that this suffering is temporary but your joy is eternal.

Saved

> "I, I am the Lord, and besides me there is no savior.
> I declared and saved and proclaimed,
> when there was no strange god among you;
> and you are my witnesses," declares the Lord,
> "and I am God."
>
> Isaiah 43:11-12 esv

When the drudgery of life wears down my defenses and I am left feeling vulnerable and raw, God, what should my response be? Do I just try harder? Do I hunker down and keep going, hoping that at some point things will change? Unless I have help, there is certainly little hope for transformation.

When my reserves are tapped, I can't be expected to thrive. God, you are the source of every good thing and you never run out or run dry. You are the help I need and the Savior that continually comes through for me. Where I feel overwhelmed and under fire on every side, I call out to you, my faithful God, who rescues me.

Faithful One, I depend on you for help in every trouble I face. I cannot save myself. You know how I've tried! Don't stop showing off in power, and please don't ever stop reaching out in mercy. I am yours. Fill my heart with the confidence of your closeness.

Tired

I'm exhausted! My life is spent with sorrow,
my years with sighing and sadness.
Because of all these troubles,
I have no more strength.
My inner being is so weak and frail.

PSALM 31:10 TPT

Father, you do not shy away from the reality of my life or neglect the weariness that can erode my hope. You are not afraid of my big emotions, and you don't require me to get it all together before I come to you. You are the source where I will find the refreshing I am so desperate for.

Sometimes I am so tired and sadness is a constant companion. God, you do not promise a pain-free existence, but you vow to comfort me and empower me. Where my strength is depleted, I invite your presence to cover me with your love. You will not fail to meet me with the power of your nearness. Your love is better than anything else I can taste or experience in this world. May your compassion be my comfort and my deepest delight.

Merciful God, meet me in my weakness and empower me with your Spirit. You refresh me when I am completely depleted. Do it again, Lord.

Fulfilled Hope

Oh that I might have my request,
and that God would fulfill my hope.

JOB 6:8 ESV

Some days, God, I have confident expectation of your faithful witness in my life, and other days I struggle to believe that I will see your goodness at all. I am so thankful that your faithfulness is not dependent on my faith. You are constant and unchanging no matter what is or isn't my present reality.

I want my heart to take courage in your loyalty to your Word. You have not failed your children, and you won't fail me. Though troubles and trials come, your promise is not thrown off track. You are the fulfiller of dreams. I submit my heart to you again, when I am full of hope and when I am desperately hanging on to a thread of it. You will prove true to me. Your tender mercy is mine in every moment.

Good God, even when I struggle to hope, you remain constant. What a relief that I can't talk you out of your faithfulness. I give you access to my heart again, and ask that you would breathe peace, hope, and love into my being. As I wait on you, I will find strength. You meet me in the middle of every moment.

Trust

Preserve me, O God,
for in you I put my trust.

PSALM 16:1 NKJV

God, what does active trust look like? Is it blind hope that keeps its fingers crossed throughout the hard times? Is it a continual surrender of my own control and belief that you will stay true to your nature? It is so much more than a one-time statement of faith. As I practice placing my hope in you, my confidence will grow as you continue to show up in faithfulness.

You are a refuge to those who seek shelter in your name. You preserve and keep me safe in your mercy. What you give to me no one and nothing can take away—no storm, no evil person, no hateful act, no betrayal. You are dependable in compassion and reliable in love.

Father, I continually put my trust in you. You know my heart and how it fluctuates, but I am grateful that you never change even when I do. Meet me with your loyal love and fill me with everything I need for today.

Radiant Hope

The Lord alone is our radiant hope
and we trust in him with all our hearts.
His wrap-around presence will strengthen us.

PSALM 33:22 TPT

When nothing seems to be going right, and I am overwhelmed by all that needs to be done, it can be hard not to spiral in worry, Father. But you are my sure help in every season. When I rely on my own limited strategies to get me through, it will only take me so far. Your wisdom is better, and it is the perfect solution to every problem I encounter.

In my weakness, God, you meet me with the power of your presence and strengthen me. Your Spirit wraps around me with the warmth of your love that embraces me. I find my hope in this place; you are the sweetest treasure in this life. Your goodness is ever increasing; I have not seen the end of it. Help me to trust you with all of my heart.

Lord, fill my heart with hope as I look to you. You surround me with your presence and my heart comes alive. I want to know you more today. Encourage my soul in the way that only you can.

Words of Hope

I rise before dawn and cry for help;
I put my hope in your words.

PSALM 119:147 NRSV

God, in the restlessness of endless thoughts that won't quit, worry sometimes leads me to sleepless nights. When I cannot calm my mind, I have access to you, the giver of all peace. Your presence is pure love; you comfort me in the middle of my mess, whether in the dark of night or the bright day light. You are always available.

When I am struggling to find peace, I want to look into your Word to find hope in your faithful character. You have never failed, and you won't start now. I cry out for help and I listen for your reply. You will answer me because you are not silent. When it is hard to hear, I look for the mercy and kindness I may have been resisting. It is clearly laid out in your Word. Help me to seek and find it.

God, you are my hope. I rely solely on you for the help I need. Come into the craziness of my circumstances and calm every fear with the faithful way you work. I trust that you have not left me alone. You are with me in the joys and the sorrows. Turn around what looks impossible and mark my life with your goodness.

One Thing

I have not achieved it,
but I focus on this one thing:
Forgetting the past
and looking forward
to what lies ahead.

PHILIPPIANS 3:13 NLT

Father, I have not reached the end of my hope. As long as I draw breath into my lungs, my story is not finished. When I get caught up in the shame of my past and can't see a way to move forward, I may struggle to believe that your redemptive power can make my future better. But that is simply not the truth!

Is my focus in life to be amazing at my job, or to be present with my family, or to get a degree? God, I know these are all great pursuits, but they are limited in their scope. With you as my main goal, knowing that your kingdom will come and your will be done on earth as it is in heaven, my hopes will be fulfilled.

Jesus, you are the one that I am running after in this life. Even as I run, I realize that through your presence in the Spirit, you are with me. I look to you for everything I need; I'm desperate for you to turn around what I have made a mess of. Come do what only you can do.

February

Look to the LORD and his strength;
seek his face always.

1 CHRONICLES 16:11 NIV

Loved

Cast all your anxiety on him
because he cares for you.

1 PETER 5:7 NRSV

God, there is such a difference between sharing my troubles with someone I barely know and sharing them with a trusted friend. Sometimes I struggle to know which category you fall into when I need to unload my concerns.

Help me to know there is safety in this relationship because I am loved by you. I don't need to question your intentions toward me. Your love and care for me is greater than the expanse of the universe. I cannot reach the end of it because there is none. I give my worries to you. You love me better than anyone else can.

Loving Father, I give you my anxiety today. I don't want to carry it on my own any longer. Wrap me in your great love that casts out every fear and cover me with your peace that transcends my understanding.

Supported

"Don't worry, because I am with you.
Don't be afraid, because I am your God.
I will make you strong and will help you;
I will support you with my right hand that saves you."

ISAIAH 41:10 NCV

In my weakness, it is wise to lean on the support you provide, God. It is not failure to be helped. It is the reinforcement that causes me to be strengthened. When I think through those who have exhibited great faith, it isn't that they did great things on their own—that has never been the plot.

Abraham, Moses, Daniel, and Mary are a few examples of those who lived with perseverance. They also lived out incredible supernatural experiences, none of which were based on their own abilities. The things I am facing now that seem impossible pale in comparison to their trials! I am not being thrown into a lion's den, or leaving for an unknown destination, or leading a nation of people into a desert. Thank you, God, that my fear can be turned to faith when I lean on your undeniable, inexhaustible strength.

Almighty God, I so often lose sight of your incredible faithfulness to those who call on you. I am yours, and I believe that even if I can't see how you will turn my circumstances around, you are with me every step of the way.

Here Now

> "Do not worry about tomorrow;
> for tomorrow will care for itself.
> Each day has enough trouble of its own."
>
> MATTHEW 6:34 NASB

The flowers of the field do not work and yet they bloom in beauty, Father. The birds of the air are not responsible to produce their own food, and still you provide everything they need. How much more will you provide everything I need today?

Help me to let go of the unknowns that produce worry over my life. I release them to you today. This is a fresh opportunity to embrace what is in front of me. What can I do? Who should I love? I leave tomorrow in your hands and embrace the present. I want my perspective to be changed.

Lord, I am grateful to know that you are not far off in the future. You are always present in every moment. I let go of the worries I've been carrying around and trust that as you always have so you will continue to provide for me and those I love.

Trust Jesus

"Don't worry or surrender to your fear.
For you've believed in God,
now trust and believe in me also."

JOHN 14:1 TPT

Jesus, you reflect your Father to the world. You are the tangible representation of love. Perfect love, as it says in first John, that drives out fear. You laid down your very life to reveal the length that God would go for me to be reunited with him in love.

Where there is fear that threatens to overshadow the goodness in my life, I accept your invitation to trust and believe that your love knows no limitations. Love me to life again and again, if that's what it takes. Your grace is not transactional; it is not dependent on what I have to offer.

Great God, I don't want to be overrun by fear anymore. Where worry and dread have closed me in, I ask for your grace to tear down the walls and bring freedom. I trust you, Jesus, to surprise me with your love again.

Call Out

From the depths of despair, O Lord,
I call for your help.

PSALM 130:1 NLT

God, when anxiety builds like a pressure-cooker as thoughts race around my mind, desperation sometimes takes over. In the spiral, when it feels like everything is out-of-control, what should I do?

When I have exhausted my own resources, I must rely on others. You are my ultimate help though. When I feel isolated and alone, you are with me. You also created me for community. I was not meant to simply survive on my own; I was always meant to be part of a family. Wherever I find myself today, I know that help is within reach.

Jehovah, you are the keeper of all my days. When I come to the end of myself, I find that you have always been more than enough. Help me today in my desperation. I cannot save myself.

Strong Love

The LORD is my light and my salvation—
whom shall I fear?
The LORD is the stronghold of my life—
of whom shall I be afraid?

PSALM 27:1 NIV

In the storms of life, God, your truth shines like a lighthouse, beckoning me to the safety of your love. You are like a fortified castle where I can take shelter and receive protection from the attack of the enemy. You are stronger than any weapon both formed and imagined. Your love is strong enough to keep me safe.

When fear threatens to cripple me and it sends my mind spinning, help me to turn to you. I want to find refuge in the covering of your love. Fight my battles for me as I take rest in you. Be the foundation that grounds me. Your perfect love covers me, calming my anxieties and feelings of distress.

Loving God, I ask for your powerful love to calm all my anxious thoughts today. You are the shelter where I hide. I have no strength to fight, Lord. Be my defender!

Unashamed

Hope does not put us to shame,
because God's love has been poured into our hearts
through the Holy Spirit who has been given to us.

ROMANS 5:5 ESV

God, when things don't go my way, or I end up in situations that highlight my shortcomings, discouragement sets in. Disappointment turns to shame when I see these things attached to my worth. I feel like a failure. Thank you that even though I fall short time and time again, I am not defined by my failures.

My true worth is found in my belonging to you, Father. I bear the resemblance of you. I am not worthless. I am continually loved to life by you—the source of all that is good and true. You are my present help in times of trouble, and you will never leave me.

Ever-present One, pour your love into me again today with the sweetness of your presence. Remove all the residue of shame that has turned scars into character flaws; lift the weight of discouragement and fill me with hope again.

Safe and Secure

You will have confidence,
because there is hope;
you will be protected
and take your rest in safety.

JOB 11:18 NRSV

Father, I know that children in healthy families are confident of their parents' ability to keep them safe and secure. They are not required to fend for themselves because everything they need is taken care of. Loving parents protect their families and their kids take comfort in the leadership they provide.

Whether or not this is what I experienced as a child, I can rest in the knowledge that I am being cared for, provided for, and protected by you. I am not left on my own to figure things out. My confidence is in you, my ever-present God, who doesn't miss a detail. I can yield the unknown to you, trusting that you see and provide for all I need.

Faithful Father, I trust that you will continue to take care of me as you have up until now. You are not absent. I have confidence in your goodness and I can rest in you, knowing that you don't miss a thing.

Words of Promise

Remember the word to Your servant,
Upon which You have caused me to hope.

PSALM 119:49 NKJV

Your Word, God, is full of examples of your faithfulness. You are a keeper of promises. You don't change your mind. You speak and then you act (even if it's not always in the timeline I want). All of your promises can be counted on because they depend on your very character.

I am so grateful for your promises that bring me hope. They are tied to the truth of who you are. You are not a liar and you can never become one. Encourage my heart today in the knowledge that you are a keeper of your word, and it is in your Word that I hope.

God of truth, I take hope in the knowledge that your word is sincere. You are faithful and true, and I trust in you. Where I have been disappointed, let my heart be encouraged in seeing you come through in better ways than I could have ever expected.

Keep Praying

One day Jesus taught the apostles to keep praying
and never stop or lose hope.

LUKE 18:1 TPT

When I call out to you, Jesus, I am teaching my heart to
turn to you. As I continually pray and communicate with
you, I can't help but be changed by the awareness that you
are bigger than my circumstances. You are bigger than my
small life can contain.

You taught your disciples to pray, not just as something to
do, but because it was how you communicated with the
Father. Your life was a beautiful example of how to stay
connected with God, no matter what situations you faced.
As you lived, so I want to live—with hopeful expectation.

Father, let love be the fuel to my life. When I am
discouraged, help me to keep looking to you. I won't stop
praying. Fill me with your hope again today.

Whole Heart

A happy heart is like good medicine,
but a broken spirit drains your strength.

PROVERBS 17:22 NCV

God, you bind up the brokenhearted. You take what seems irreparable and make it completely new. Where I am broken and hurting, I invite you to minister to me with the life of your presence. You bring into being what never existed. You will not let me be crushed.

I look to you for healing today. You have not forgotten me. Take my broken pieces and make me whole. I find my hope in you. Come and fill me up with immeasurable grace that empowers me to thrive and not just survive. You are my strength. I lift my eyes to you.

Lord, where I have been struggling to just get through, come in and breathe new life that revives my soul. I have no hope apart from you. You are everything. With expectation, I invite you to do what only you can do: make my heart whole in your love. Nothing else will do.

Steady Ground

Every valley shall be raised up,
every mountain and hill made low;
the rough ground shall become level,
the rugged places a plain.

ISAIAH 40:4 NIV

Father, there are many peaks and valleys as I walk through life. When I expect a continually smooth road, somewhere along the way my hope will be disappointed. You are faithful to be the firm foundation in my life. You never change. When everything that can be shaken is shaken, I find that I am still standing on you, my Rock.

When my hope is in you and not the details of my life, I find the courage to trust you no matter what is going on. One day there will be no more need for faith in what I cannot see because everything will be made clear. Until that day, help me to keep trusting in you because you never waver.

Faithful One, my heart takes hope in the reality that you never change. You are my strength when I am weak, my shelter in the storms of life, and my joy in the middle of suffering. Lead me on in your love, Lord, and bring me into freedom so that even when I am walking through the valley, I am full of your presence.

Joyful Surrender

Taste and see that the LORD is good.
Oh, the joys of those who take refuge in him!

PSALM 34:8 NLT

God, at times I am overcome with the joy of knowing you and your goodness. I know that your affection over me can bring me freedom. I take refuge in you and ask you to take care of what I cannot. The fruit of your kingdom is that which brings life to my soul: it is love, joy, peace, and kindness.

Today is the perfect opportunity to lay down my burdens at your feet. You are my God and my King. I ask you to do the heavy lifting. As I rest in you, help me to find the restoration that my weary soul has been longing for. I want to taste and see that you are good today, Lord.

Good God, you are my safe place of refuge. I bring you every worry, care, and burden that has been weighing me down. I lay them at your feet today. As I exchange my heavy burdens for your light ones, I am able to breathe deeply again. What a relief! You are my freedom and my joy.

Higher Love

Your lovingkindness, O LORD,
extends to the heavens,
Your faithfulness reaches to the skies.

PSALM 36:5 NASB

There is no limit to your love, God. It is so much sweeter, so much better, than any love I could experience this side of heaven. Your intentions are pure. Your heart toward me is full of fiery love that does not belittle or make me feel less than anyone or anything. Your love lifts the lonely; it is extravagantly poured out at every opportunity.

You cannot be understood apart from your deep affection because your very nature is love. You are not a dictator, requiring me to fall in line because you said so. You love me to life at every turn with kindness and gentleness. Even your correction is laced with love. Your love is abundantly available to me in every moment, including right now.

Loving God, give me a fresh revelation of the depth of your affection today. Where it has felt stale, breathe new insight into the depths of my heart, opening my eyes to the greatness of your love. You are better than I expect at every turn. Thank you for your great mercy that covers me all the days of my life.

Dependable

The word of the LORD is upright,
and all his work is done in faithfulness.

PSALM 33:4 ESV

Father, many of us grow up in families where we learn to depend on ourselves for our needs. Even if that was not my situation and I came from a stable family, I have found a way to cope with various circumstances by withdrawing and seeking solutions where my needs have been left unmet. I know this is not the model I am supposed to live by.

You are a good Father. You are always available and you meet every need. You are dependable and trustworthy. I don't have to figure things out on my own; I don't have to suffer through the consequences of my circumstances in isolation. I was created to lean on your help. I will never outgrow my status as your child. I take the opportunity that today provides to ask for help when I need it. You lovingly intervene for my benefit and I am so grateful.

Lord, I humbly offer you my heart today. See where I fall short; I so easily do! I need your help, God, and I don't want to keep striving in my own strength. You always know better than I do. I lean into your loyal love today, knowing I will receive help whenever I need it.

Protected

The Lord is faithful,
who will establish you
and guard you from the evil one.

2 THESSALONIANS 3:3 NKJV

God, when I feel lost to my circumstances, nearly drowning in the worries of this world, there is a place of refuge available in you. My rescuer, you will not let me be crushed by my situation. You are faithful to save me every single time. You are my protector and the guardian of my soul. I ask you to remove every lie that stands between me and the freedom of your intentions toward me to come crashing down today.

I have been found by you, my faithful Father. You never hesitate in your affections for me. The love of the father of the prodigal son is just a glimpse into your goodness toward your children. Where I have wondered about my worth, I ask for your love to wash over me in abundance. You always pick me up and welcome me into your warm embrace with joy.

Faithful One, you are the one I lean on. I depend on you to guard and protect me from the evil one. Love of God, flood my mind, my heart, and my body today. I receive the kindness of your heart. I am yours. May I forever be found in you.

Firmly Planted

To all who mourn in Israel,
he will give a crown of beauty for ashes,
a joyous blessing instead of mourning,
festive praise instead of despair.
In their righteousness, they will be like great oaks
that the Lord has planted for his own glory.

ISAIAH 61:3 NLT

God, you are close to those who mourn. You meet me in the middle of my sorrow. But you don't stop there. You promise to give me beauty for ashes, joy instead of mourning, celebratory praise instead of despair. I am firmly planted in your love.

I do not despair in my mourning. I know you don't expect me to pretend that things are better than they are. I don't need to will myself to be positive. You are my source. You are the initiator of this great exchange. You will not leave me on my own, and I will not be lost to the anguish of my soul. You have planted me in your kingdom and I know you will tend to me.

Merciful God, I am so thankful for your presence that never leaves. I trust that you are right here with me in every moment. Increase my awareness of your closeness. Cover me with your love and lift my head to see your goodness today.

Keep Asking

Do not worry about anything,
but pray and ask God for everything you need,
always giving thanks.

PHILIPPIANS 4:6 NCV

God, you don't weary of my questions or my wonderings.
Like a patient father, you welcome my musings and
my quirky thoughts at every opportunity. You are not
ambivalent toward me. You delight in my asking. You never
turn away from my open heart no matter what is spilling out.

I don't want to censor myself with you. I ask you for
everything I need. I don't hold back even my doubts. You
can handle them, and I don't need to keep them bottled
up. With the gratefulness of a heart that is openly received,
I won't stop myself from airing out the corners of my mind
with you. How you delight in communion with me!

Provider, I will not hesitate to freely come to you with
everything on my mind today. I am so thankful that your
heart is open and your ears are attentive to me. I will not
stop myself from asking and seeking for fear that you will
grow tired of me. I will train my mind to be freely open
with you today. Thank you, Lord!

Wasted Energy

"Can any one of you by worrying
add a single hour to your life?"

MATTHEW 6:27 NIV

When life gets overwhelming, God, my mind runs away
with all the possibilities of what could happen. When I
don't know how something will turn out, it can be second
nature for me to worry about it. As you said in your Word,
worry doesn't add a single hour to my life.

You are all-seeing and all-knowing. It is not wishful
thinking to trust you to guide me through every hill and
valley. Where confusion clouds my understanding, you
are completely confident. I lean on you and your wisdom
today. You won't let me down.

Great God, I am so grateful that you are not confused by
anything. I remind myself that you are above it all. I trust
you today; I align myself with your truth and your wisdom.
I'm leaning on you. When I am tempted to worry, I will turn
that energy toward trusting you.

Able

Can any idols of the nations bring rain?
Or can the heavens give showers?
Is it not you, O Lᴏʀᴅ our God?
We set our hope on you,
for it is you who do all this.

Jᴇʀᴇᴍɪᴀʜ 14:22 ɴʀsᴠ

Father God, you are able to do all that I could ever think or imagine and so much more! You are the hope that holds me together when everything around me is falling apart. You are the source of every good thing. You never stop working, never pause your plans, and you do not grow weary of faithfully showing up in love.

What would it look like for me to align myself in complete and total trust of you, my Maker? What would happen if I gave myself fully to believing that you would come through just like you said you would? Your track record is impeccable. You do not fail. Let my hope be firmly planted in you, my faithful God.

Lord of heaven and earth, who is there like you? You are faithful beyond all measure. Who can count the ways that you reveal your lovingkindness to your people? Show up again in power, Lord. I put all my hope and trust in you!

All I Need

"The Lord is my portion," says my soul,
"therefore I will hope in him."

LAMENTATIONS 3:24 ESV

There is no need I have that is met outside of your grace,
God. You are the portion I crave, and you are so satisfying.
Where I see the unmet desires of my heart, there is space
for your provision. You do not delight in my anxiety, nor do
you take satisfaction in my disappointment.

Your heart is full of abundance for every longing I have.
You are the giver of good gifts and the fulfillment of the
joy I crave. Help me to find my heart's desire met in your
fullness. May my hope be found in you, for surely you will
not let me down.

Lord, you are my portion. Everything I need is found in
you, and I come with expectation today to receive out of
the fullness of your heart. I rely on you. You alone are my
confidence.

Deliverance Is Coming

"Keep your hope to the end
and you will experience life and deliverance."

MATTHEW 24:13 TPT

In the waiting, it can be hard not to grow discouraged, Father. I know this is where my attention matters. I want to fellowship with those who help me and lift me up, not plug along with the disheartened and discouraged. I know there is a place for sharing in suffering, but the messages I receive from media, faithless friends, and society at large affect me negatively.

Am I feeding my soul with the despair of the world or the hope of your kingdom? I cannot escape the harsh realities of life, but I can take ownership of the messages I allow into my home and my heart. You are my hope and you are my deliverer. I want to align myself with your love, displayed in your Word and in fellowship with others who are submitted to your grace.

God, as I cling to your Word, I know that life and deliverance are coming. Even as I wait on you, I choose to continue to believe in hope that you are coming and you will restore all that has been lost. You are consistently good, and I choose to trust in your goodness.

Shared Comfort

Our hope for you is firmly grounded,
knowing that as you are sharers of our sufferings,
so also you are sharers of our comfort.

2 CORINTHIANS 1:7 NASB

There is encouragement in the experience of sharing in another's burdens, God. When I don't have to carry a heavy load alone, I am filled with courage and strength to keep going. I was not meant to bear my heaviness alone. This was never a part of your design. You created us for fellowship.

When you created Adam, you did not stop there. You declared that it was not good for man to be alone, so you made a companion in Eve. This was the blueprint at the beginning, and it is still the standard. I was made for relationship—for family. As I share in the sufferings of others, so do I share in their comfort.

Father, I see you in the beauty of community. Your Word says that you set the lonely in families. Where I have been alone and isolated, I ask that you would give me the fellowship I crave. Your heart is shown clearly in relationship; it's what I was made for. Thank you for your comfort in people around me. Help me to stay connected!

Sincere Hope

We desire each one of you to show the same
earnestness to have the full assurance of hope
until the end.

HEBREWS 6:11 ESV

When my hope is in you, God, it is not frivolous or wishful thinking. You are the same God who raises the dead to life and completes the work you began in me. Belief in you is not a fad, nor does it prove to be unfruitful. When the going gets tough, help me to continue to turn my eyes to you and press into your faithful love. I don't want to walk away in disappointment.

Encourage my heart to understand that the hope I have is not based on the happiness I may or may not feel in any moment. In the darkest night, you are with me. You are steadfast and secure. I will not be tricked into thinking that if I don't feel good about how my life is going, then I must not be cut out for faith. My confidence is found in your steady nature instead!

Faithful One, I set my thoughts on your character today. May my heart be full of courage to keep believing and trusting that you will never fail. I rely on you and on your love.

Hold On

Let us hold fast the confession of our hope
without wavering, for He who promised is faithful.

HEBREWS 10:23 NASB

Your nature, God, is far beyond any good character I could ever exhibit in my life. Your faithfulness never fails. Not once. Your loyal love never hesitates. It is always flowing, never receding. There is no need for you to ask for forgiveness because you are perfect in all your ways: the ways I understand and those I don't.

Help me not to be foolish enough to think that I know better than you. Let me ascribe to you what belongs to you—the praise and gratefulness you deserve. As I do, my heart will be turned to you in adoration. Not everything that happens in my life is from you. I want to remember that there is an enemy that seeks to steal, kill, and destroy. Help me to hold fast to my hope in you, the King of love who never betrays his character.

God over all, I have seen your faithfulness in my life; even now as I look, I see it! May my heart be bound to yours in love that all my days I would stay tucked into your mercy, clinging to who you are. Thank you for relationship with you; you are beautiful in all your ways!

Patient Endurance

You also keep your hopes high and be patient,
for the presence of the Lord is drawing closer.

JAMES 5:8 TPT

God, just as a farmer waits patiently for his harvest,
knowing that nature needs to run its course, so I want to
remember that I am waiting for a coming King who will
appear in the proper time. The farmer does what he knows
to do, but he cannot speed up the harvest.

In the same way, my hope is set on a promise that will be
fulfilled through your return. Though the waiting is long,
to my standards, the time is coming. As I linger in the in-
between space, I choose to do what I am called to do, all
the while being confident that the harvest is sure to come.
Even as I wait, I have your presence with me, filling me with
courage, joy, peace, and the abundance of your love.

Yahweh, you are the God who was, who is, and who always
will be. I have placed all my bets on you; let my heart be
convinced of your goodness and faithfulness. Holy Spirit,
fill me with the love that fuels my freedom. You are my joy
and my great reward!

Mindful Discipline

Prepare your minds for action; discipline yourselves;
set all your hope on the grace that Jesus Christ
will bring you when he is revealed.

1 PETER 1:13 NRSV

Father, living by faith is not circumstantial, and it is
not produced by accident. Faith is an active choosing
to believe in something or someone. In the world of
spirituality, discipline can get a bad rap. However, when I
look into the practice of spiritual disciplines, they benefit
my faith by training me to align to your kingdom ways.

Help me not to float along in my faith. I want to regulate
my mind and actions in partnership with your Spirit. There
is no condemnation or judgment for where I am today. I
take hope in the grace that you freely give to empower
me to live liberated in your law of love. I direct my heart
toward you through your Word and in prayer.

Holy One, you freely give to all those who ask for help
in your name. Fill me with your grace that gives me the
strength to live aligned with your life and light. May the
boundaries of my heart be expanded, even as I actively
restrict where my attentions go. You are worthy of my
obedience!

Don't Give Up

Though He slay me, I will hope in Him.
Nevertheless I will argue my ways before Him.

JOB 13:15 NASB

When life's circumstances are grim and confusing, it is hard not to believe that even you, God, are against me. But that is not your nature. You are a wrap-around shield to those who take refuge in you. Though my situation doesn't always line up with your character, your presence fills me with what I need—even in the face of tragedy and sorrow.

I want to continue to hope in you when everything seems to be falling apart. As I struggle to sense your goodness, I dare to cling to you even then. I risk depending on you even when those around me give up. If the mountains fall into the sea and the nations rage against each other, you are still the same merciful, all-powerful God you always were.

Merciful Father, I bind my heart to yours in hope today. Give me confidence as I walk in your way of love. Even as I press on, I ask that you would give me the tenacity to hold onto you no matter what. I believe, Lord, help my unbelief!

March

We are confident
that he hears us
whenever we ask for
anything that pleases him.

<small>1 John 5:14 NLT</small>

Fulfillment

He will not ignore forever all the needs of the poor,
for those in need shall not always be crushed.
Their hopes shall be fulfilled, for God sees it all!

PSALM 9:18 TPT

God of all creation, full of both power and kindness, you will not turn a blind eye to anyone in need. When I feel alone in my struggle, I can find rest in you because you see it all. I will not be crushed by these momentary troubles that burden me.

Today I choose to feel hope for my life. I take this moment to recall your faithfulness, God. When I have been overwhelmed by fear and overcome with worry in the past, marinating in those feelings did not help me at all. Some days feel like too much to bear, but I will invite your presence to breathe hope into me again. I shake off the dust of the pressures that are beyond me and I give them to you.

Powerful One, I trust in your Word that says I am not alone in my struggles. You see everything, and I am known by you. Remind me again of your faithfulness and encourage my heart to hope in you.

Good God

The LORD is good to those whose hope is in him,
to the one who seeks him.

LAMENTATIONS 3:25 NIV

Father, I can find hope when I press into your goodness. Some days, and even some seasons, it is difficult to practice this. When circumstances are confusing and cycles of shame seem unending, I forget what your goodness tastes like.

Help me not to wait until I feel better to seek you, Lord. I don't want to hide from you or ignore the pull of your presence because I'm upset with you. There is nothing that is too much for you. Not my doubts, worries, anger, or fear. I bring them all to you today and taste your kindness. You lead in love and you will not condemn my heart when it seeks your truth.

Father, I come to you today with all that I've been holding back. I cannot hide the state of my heart from you, and I don't want to. Here I am, Lord. Here is all I have. Speak your better word over my life today. I need to hear from your heart.

Morning Is Coming

That time of darkness and despair
will not go on forever.

ISAIAH 9:1 NLT

Father God, sometimes I experience the inevitable dark nights of my soul. Grief is unavoidable; I am acquainted with loss. The deep sorrow that fills me when I mourn both great and seemingly invisible losses is not something I can wish myself out of. Jesus, you knew this well as the Man of Sorrows. You are familiar with suffering and anguish. I do not need to hide this part of myself from you.

Knowing that you know it all and see it through your eyes of love, I approach you with my broken heart. I trust you to care for me, and even to carry me, through the times when I have nothing to offer. You promise that the morning is coming.

Ever-present One, I have to believe that when the sun rises on my dark night, I will see evidence of your goodness that was with me all along. I offer you myself though it's not much. I am grateful that you love me for me and not for what I can do for you. Hold me near, Lord. I need you.

Fed by Love

He has brought me to his banquet hall,
And his banner over me is love.

SONG OF SOLOMON 2:4 NASB

You have prepared a place for me at your banqueting table, God. I am not welcomed in as a stranger but as a friend. My place will not be filled by another—it is mine alone. I see how you welcome me with affection. I can come as I am and feast on your love.

I don't have to clean myself up to come to you. You will rain over me with your lovingkindness and lighten my load with your warm embrace. Your refreshing presence will assure me of the delight I bring to you. Thank you for loving and accepting me just as I am.

Loving Father, I want to know your thoughts toward me today. Help me to see what you see without the shame and worthlessness that has been clouding my thoughts. Your love is strong enough to hold every part of my world; help me to let go of control and trust that you really are all I need.

Spirit Fruit

God will never give you the spirit of fear,
but the Holy Spirit who gives you
mighty power, love, and self-control.

1 TIMOTHY 1:7 TPT

What a wonderful gift I've been given in you, Holy Spirit, who fills me, guides me, and empowers me to live as Christ did. I know that when I am filled with fear that immobilizes me, it is not from you. Rather, you are full of love, grace, strength, and peace.

When the frenzy of fear has me feeling like I need to make hasty decisions in order to right what is off kilter in my life, it is an opportunity to slow down, take a breath, and gauge the source. You do not create anxiety in my heart. You give me peace that calms the storm within me.

Holy Spirit, I am so grateful for your presence in my life. Even when I can't sense you, I know that you are with me. Fill me with your peace that calms my anxious thoughts and worried heart. Do what only you can do and change me from the inside out.

Confident Perseverance

Do not throw away your confidence,
which has a great reward.

HEBREWS 10:35 NCV

When winter comes, I find myself faced with a new rhythm, Creator God. Nature shows me that there are cycles to life. In the slowdown of winter, when the days are shorter, I can rest assured that it won't last forever. When spring breaks and I see new life sprouting up everywhere, it is a reminder of the rebirth that comes out of every dark season.

My dark, cold winter of the soul will also end and I will experience the rebirth of spring again. Whatever season I find myself in, I can be confident that it won't last forever. I will not despair if my winter has felt long. New life is coming. It is on the way. I will see the goodness of my God in the land of the living.

Steady One, I lean into your wisdom today. I trust that I will see the beauty of new life springing, even if all I see now is barrenness. Uplift my heart today, God, with hope. Lighten the weight of unmet expectations as I lift my eyes to you.

Continue to Believe

These things I have written to you who believe in the name of the Son of God, that you may know that you have eternal life, and that you may continue to believe in the name of the Son of God.

1 JOHN 5:13 NKJV

Jesus, my Savior, I have yielded my life to you. Because of this, I can be sure that I will receive the fruit that living a life for you brings. The nearness of the Holy Spirit who comforts, guides, and heals is mine for all my days. I will not give up hope when life takes a turn. Troubles come and go, but they are not the final word over my life.

As a believer, my hope is not limited to this short time on earth—it is so much greater! I have eternal life with you waiting on the other side. Help me to press on believing that you are who you say you are. Your faithfulness will never come to an end. I can rest in the assurance of my place in your kingdom.

Son of God, in you is the fulfillment of every promise. Your love is constant and true, and it is persistently covering me all the days of my life. I choose to continue to believe in you. You are better than I can even comprehend. Thank you for your faithfulness.

Come Boldly

Let us come boldly to the throne of our gracious God.
There we will receive his mercy, and we will find grace
to help us when we need it most.

HEBREWS 4:16 NLT

As a child of yours, Father, I have access to your presence.
When Jesus died and the veil inside the temple that
kept the people from the holy of holies was torn, every
hindrance that could keep me from you was removed. I can
come shamelessly into your presence, knowing that I will
be met by your kindness.

There is nothing that can keep me from your love and
mercy. I boldly enter your presence, bringing all that I am
before you. There I will find the strength I need and the
grace that empowers me to live out what I could never
do on my own. Why would I try to fight my way into your
good standing when I have free access just as I am?

Merciful One, I approach you confidently, knowing that I am
welcome in whatever state I come. Meet me with your love,
filling me with the grace I so desperately need. You are the
source of everything I'm longing for. I need you. Thank you
for always accepting me as I am. I belong to you.

Power to Stand

Be strong in the Lord and in his mighty power.
Put on the full armor of God,
so that you can take your stand
against the devil's schemes.

EPHESIANS 6:10-11 NIV

When I am out of my depth and don't know how to move forward, I find that desperation quickly leads to a sense of being overwhelmed, God. Even the best problem solvers in the world are limited by their scope of understanding. Thank you that you don't expect me to fight my battles in my own strength, relying on my limited resources.

In your mighty power, I can find ultimate strength. You have given me instructions for life and for the battles that rage in teaching me to wear your armor. Clothed in faith, truth, holiness, the power of salvation, and the readiness of the gospel of peace, I will be covered for everything I face. I will find the power to stand my ground as I lean into your wisdom.

Wise God, you have given me everything I need to thrive in life. I will not neglect your Word as I face the battles before me. I cannot fight in my own strength; if I did, I would be beaten down time and again. I rely on you, God. You are my strength and the light of my life.

Possibility

"All things are possible
to him who believes."

MARK 9:23 NASB

Father, when I am in a privileged place in life, things feel easy. But I know I will still face inevitable hardship. When I am struggling to make it through the days, weeks, and months, it can be a battle to hope for better. Jesus faced the trials and struggles that I do, and yet he never wavered in faith.

I want to be found full of faith like Abraham who waited for the promise of his son far longer than he expected. I want to press on in the face of what looks like barrenness. I want to trust your Word when it seems impossible like Mary did when the angel told her she was going to mother the Son of God. Your ways are mysterious, but your faithfulness is not a guessing game!

All-powerful God, I want to be perseverant in faith even when everything in my life looks like it goes against your promises. Help me to cling to you, knowing that you are faithful to your Word every time. You have not changed who you are, and I can trust in your unfailing love to cover me every step of the journey of my life.

Living God

To this end we toil and strive,
because we have our hope set on the living God,
who is the Savior of all people,
especially of those who believe.

HEBREWS 6:11 ESV

God, you are the same yesterday, today, and forever. When I consider the works of your hands, the miracles you have displayed, the wonders of your glorious love, may my heart be encouraged to press on in hope. You have not grown silent, and you have not stopped working. You are as alive today as you were when Jesus walked the earth. You are as faithful today as you were to Abraham and Moses.

Your ways are mysterious to me because I only see and know in part. You see all and know all. You understand the whole picture and you are intimately aware of the minute details. My heart can find courage as I trust your wisdom over my own. May I continue to walk in your power and love, my living God, who is present with me in the middle of every moment!

Living God, you are incredibly patient and kind with me. I find myself wanting my heart to believe in confidence that you are who you say you are. Fill me with your presence that calms my anxious fears and stills my chaotic thoughts. You are my portion.

All I Have

I cried out to you, Lord, my only hiding place.
You're all I have, my only hope in this life,
my last chance for help.

PSALM 142:5 TPT

When situations are desperate and there are no clear answers before me, I am aware of my need for you to come through, Father. When I've exhausted all my resources and I have nothing left to pull from, your help is all I'm left with. Though this feels uncomfortable, your solutions are best anyway.

Whether I find myself in a dire circumstance or the mundane of my routine, I can be sure that your help is always available to me. You are a shelter to those seeking respite from the storms of life. You are always ready to come to my aid when I ask. Help me not to hesitate to cry out to you. I know you are listening.

Lord, you are my hiding place. I rely on your help to get me through every trial. I lean into your wisdom today. Fill me with the peace of your presence that passes all understanding.

Dawn Is Coming

My soul waits for the Lord
More than the watchmen for the morning;
Indeed, more than the watchmen for the morning.

PSALM 130:6 NASB

Creator God, the darkness of night hides the beauty of the life growing all around me. There is a stillness that comes with the night, and clarity when I learn to depend on my other senses. When I find myself unable to see and confused as to what is going on, I can learn to lean into your voice. You promise to never leave me or abandon me.

The night never lasts forever; the sun always rises. So it is with the dark circumstances of life. They will not last forever. Dawn is coming. When the sun rises on this dark night of the soul, I will be able to see the life that was hidden from my sight. Your goodness has not forsaken me even in the blackest night. You promise to be with me until the end of the age. Where you are, there is life.

Faithful Friend, I take courage in your Word that promises that you won't ever leave me. I cling to the confident hope of the sun rising again, and I believe I will see your goodness in my life.

Planted

He will be strong, like a tree planted near water
that sends its roots by a stream.
It is not afraid when the days are hot;
its leaves are always green.
It does not worry in a year when no rain comes;
it always produces fruit.

JEREMIAH 17:8 NCV

The roots of my heart is firmly planted by springs of living water. This living water flows with your love, gracious God. Rooted here, my life will always grow. Even when drought comes, I draw from a source that goes under the surface and nourishes me. My heart is continually fed by your compassion; such nutrients produce fruit that cannot be hidden.

When I find that there is not much to draw on in my life nor circumstances for life and growth, I can be sure that everything I need is already provided. I am consistently nourished by your lifegiving presence. You are always near.

God, you are the source of every good and pure thing in my life. All the goodness that comes from my life has been created in the incubator of your love. May my heart continue to thrive in you even when dry seasons come. Thank you!

Joy in Comfort

When anxiety was great within me,
your consolation brought me joy.

PSALM 94:19 NIV

Thank you, Lord, that I am not left alone to be swept up by my sorrow and anxieties. In the middle of the chaos and confusion, your Spirit ministers to me with peace and comfort. Your presence is not an idea; it is the tangible experience of your nature. Your comfort covers me like a blanket. Your love fuels me like a stoked fire.

May my heart be one with yours in the communion of fellowship with the Spirit. As I invite you to move in my soul, however messy, I find that you simultaneously fill me and make space. I find the support I desire. You always know exactly what I need even before I do. As you console me, I find that my heart can rest in you.

Loving God, you are the support I desperately need. I have looked for consolation elsewhere, but nothing satisfies like you do. Meet me with your presence that floods my mind with peace and my heart with hope. I rely on you, God.

Tender Relief

Let your steadfast love become my comfort
according to your promise to your servant.

PSALM 119:76 NRSV

God, your love is like a tender kiss of mercy. You do not
force yourself on me, but you readily comfort me when
I make room for you. When I am beaten down by life's
storms, battered and bruised, I want to find the respite I so
desperately need in you.

Your loyal love is sweeter than honey; it is more comforting
than the arms of a mother. It is faithful to bind up my
broken heart and produce new life out of the rubble. No
matter the physical or emotional state I find myself in, I can
be sure that you are always near. You will wrap me up in
your reassuring presence. Fill me for every trial I face. You
alone offer the deep relief I am looking for.

Merciful God, you are full of lovingkindness to all who
come to you. I ask for the comfort of your presence to be
my portion today. I need you, Lord. Bring sweet relief as
your mercy touches my life. You are always good, and I
depend on you.

Courageous Heart

Be of good courage,
And He shall strengthen your heart,
All you who hope in the LORD.

PSALM 31:24 NKJV

Jesus, there is no easy path in life, no problem-free highway where I can bypass the suffering of this world. I cannot get through this existence avoiding the pain that inevitably touches my life. You are a refuge for the wanderer, strength to the weak, and healer of the broken.

When you ministered in the last years of your life, you were surrounded by the broken and needy. The sick came to you in droves looking for healing. You welcomed them all, and still you welcome me in my weakness. My hope is set on you, my source of strength for everything I face. I am filled with courage when you are my supply.

Creator God, I come to you with my little and my lack. I know that I won't leave your presence in the same way. God of abundance, fill me with the strength I need for today. My courage comes from you. You never turn away. You are my hope.

Trusted Father

Give us a Father's help when we face our enemies.
For to trust in any man is an empty hope.

PSALM 108:12 TPT

God, where my trust lies reveals the foundation of my life.
To trust anyone is to put my faith in them. Humans all fail
and fall short. It is an eventuality—a guarantee—that they
will not perfectly fulfill all that they hope or claim. God, you
are perfect in all your ways. You never lie, you never cheat,
and you don't change your mind. Your compassion is
longstanding, covering my imperfections with your grace.

Trusting you is a sure bet. You won't let me down, even as
I disappoint myself. You are so much better than I am. You
always offer the help I need without condition. You do not
keep an account of my wrongs or a record of what I owe.
You offer support whenever I need it without fail. My heart
takes hope in you alone.

Father, you are worthy of all my trust. You never fail or
waver. You are so good. I look to you today, and I know
you do not turn away from me in my seeking. Come and
breathe your life in my heart; you are my confident hope.

Constant Prayer

Rejoice in hope, be patient in tribulation,
be constant in prayer.

ROMANS 12:12 ESV

What a glorious mystery it is that you are available to me at all times through prayer, God of the ages. You never disengage from me. You hear every cry—both the spoken and unspoken—of my heart. I can be encouraged that you never tire of me. Though I grow weary of myself and others, you are full of kindness, mercy, and compassion when I come to you in every single moment.

I cannot catch you at a bad time. You are always listening with love. It is hard for me to comprehend the possibility of something so wonderful when I am faced with limitations everywhere I look. But you are limitless in love. You are abundant in power. You are full of light that chases darkness away. There are no shadows to be found in you. Help me never withhold or resist your wonderful love. It is the source of all the delight in my life.

Wonderful God, you who are rich in mercy and never failing in faithfulness, you are the one I turn to again and again. Today, I won't censor myself with you. I will constantly turn to you in conversation and in prayer. You are the best thing I've ever known. Be near even as I reach out to you.

Adopted

You did not receive a spirit of slavery to fall back into fear, but you have received a spirit of adoption. When we cry, "Abba! Father!" it is that very Spirit bearing witness with our spirit that we are children of God.

ROMANS 8:15-16 NRSV

What a wonderful reality I find within your kingdom, God. I have not been welcomed into an exclusive club when I yield my life to you. It is not a learning program or a restrictive sect. It is not a working relationship. I have been adopted into a family. I have the rights of a child of the living God!

It is hard to believe that I am welcomed as a dearly loved family member, not a slave or servant. The difference is not a subtle one. As a child, I have a deep relationship with you, Father, that is based on love and belonging, not on what I have to offer. You are a good father. What I have lacked in my earthly relationships does not rightly reflect the perfection found in your incomparable love.

Abba, I am reminded today that I am your child, not a servant. What a wonderful reminder! Thank you that I can come to you with everything I need. I will not fall into fear today as I approach you, my good Father. I belong to you.

Led by Love

"I will bring the blind by a way they did not know;
I will lead them in paths they have not known.
I will make darkness light before them,
and crooked places straight.
These things will I do for them and not forsake them."

ISAIAH 42:16 NKJV

When plans change and the fear of the unknown settles in, I am left with a choice. Father, I can either give into worry or choose to trust you. I cannot see the way sometimes, and that is okay. I don't need to know how everything will work out; I just need to trust that you will guide me in perfect wisdom. When my life is shrouded in the mystery of what the future will bring, give me courage to rely on you.

I want to believe that you will work everything out for my good. I know that you lead in love, not by obligation. Your affection for me runs deeper than I can imagine. I lean into your care for me today. You see everything that I cannot.

Loving God, I am grateful to be led by you. I take comfort in the knowledge that nothing is a mystery to you, nor is any circumstance too much for you to handle. Encourage my heart to hope in your resurrection power over my life.

Children of God

When the right time came, God sent his Son, born of a woman, subject to the law. God sent him to buy freedom for us who were slaves to the law, so that he could adopt us as his very own children.

GALATIANS 4:4-5 NLT

As your child, I am not a slave to rules but I am free to rule and reign with you as a coheir of your kingdom. I have been taught by you, and as I spend more time with you, I resemble you more closely. As I follow in your footsteps, I find that love's expression is diverse and beautiful.

Because you love me dearly, I can be confident in your affection for me. I can fully embrace my identity because you have loved, accepted, and nurtured me without fault. I can grow into what has been modeled to me. As a child of the living God, I am loved to life so I may love others in the same way—without condition.

Father, you are so wonderful in the way you lead. I look to you as the model I want to live my life by. Fill me with the wonder of a child as I lean into your love today.

Overwhelming Gladness

Do it again!
Those Yahweh has set free will return to Zion
and come celebrating with songs of joy!
They will be crowned with never-ending joy!
Gladness and joy will overwhelm them;
despair and depression will disappear!

ISAIAH 51:11 TPT

God, your freedom brings me overwhelming joy! When I find myself struggling to even hope for this, I join with Isaiah in declaring, "Do it again!" You are a lifter of heavy burdens and a master restorer. I am encouraged that even though I may not be living in this kind of freedom today, I can count on it coming soon. Today is not the end of my story.

When I align myself with your kingdom, I find that even in my darkest day, peace is still my portion. Your presence is the gift of heaven here and now. I am not waiting for a far-off day to know your goodness. Your presence is with me now, and it empowers me to live. I cry out for more of you. In you there is abundance of life and great joy.

Yahweh, you set the captives free and liberate those who were bound to darkness. I have tasted this freedom, and I long for more. Fill me with your gladness that causes me to celebrate. Do it again, Lord! You are worthy of all the praise I could ever offer; be glorified.

Double Portion

Return to your stronghold, O prisoners of hope;
today I declare that I will restore to you double.

ZECHARIAH 9:12 NRSV

Lord, you are my refuge and sanctuary. When I return to you, I find the rest that I need. My mind, heart, and body need a safe space where I can let my guard down. When I rest in your presence, I find there is always more than enough.

Help me to take some time to stop working for what I want and just rest and be rejuvenated. Life can get so busy it feels frantic. I was not made for this kind of pace. When I can't leisurely take my time to fill myself back up, I partner with you and you restore my hope. You return my strength because you are my source of strength. Fill me today with all you have for me.

Powerful One, you are the fortress where I retreat to find myself safe and secure. In your presence, I find that I am filled with everything I could ever need. Thank you that you don't give out of scarcity but abundance. I hide myself in your love today. You are the strength of my life.

Resolve

"Make up your mind not to worry beforehand
how you will defend yourselves."

LUKE 21:14 NIV

Worry is a temptation to try to figure out what is unknown.
God, I give into the anxiety-laden assumptive scenarios
that play out in my mind. Please help me take control of
these thought-storms before they become overwhelming.

It is natural to have what-ifs enter my mind. I can observe
these thoughts and then actively lead them by practicing
self-direction. This kind of self-control is actually a fruit of
your Spirit. Help me to rightly observe myself and to invite
your truth, which brings peace, in. When I meditate on
your Word, I find that I can differentiate between truth that
leads to life and lies that lead to confusion.

Lord, I'm so grateful for the ability to choose. Thank you
that your Word leads me to life time and again. When I am
lost in confusion and assumptions, would you bring my
attention back to your ways? You always have an answer,
and with your help, I will be ready for whatever comes.

Answer Me

I hope in You, O LORD;
You will answer, O LORD my God.

PSALM 38:15 NASB

Father God, the Psalms hold such a wide range of emotions and I can identify with most of them. You can handle all of my complicated feelings including the ups and downs of disappointment and joy. There is nothing I experience that is off-limits to you. I can freely express myself without the fear of judgment. I have a limited scope, but you see everything. I find courage in your confidence.

Sometimes I feel like I might be too much for you to handle. As I read through the Psalms, help me to bring all of myself to you without worrying that I am overwhelming you with my emotion. I know you will answer me just as you answer every cry of those who call out to you.

Lord, I come to you with everything I've been carrying. I will not hide my feelings from you today; here I am, with all my baggage. I trust that you will answer me every time I call on you. Don't let my heart sink into despair—I need you!

God My Help

Blessed is he whose help is the God of Jacob,
whose hope is in the Lord his God.

PSALM 146:5 ESV

God, you are the helper of the broken. Jacob did not live an exemplary young life—he was deceitful and greedy. But that was not the end of his story. He made peace with you, and you gave him a new name. You do not turn away the broken and needy; you do not turn a deaf ear to the desperate. When I call on you, you readily answer and clothe me with dignity.

Sometimes I feel like I am beyond the grip of your goodness. Speak your life over me so my heart finds peace with you. Thank you that you will help me no matter how chaotic the situation. You are more compassionate and powerful than I have given you credit for. I want to be changed by your love today.

God of Jacob, my heart takes hope in you. You take broken people and give them new identities. I want to be known as yours just as you are known as my God. I put all my hope in you; come and have your way in my life.

Eagerly Waiting

If we hope for what we do not see,
we eagerly wait for it with perseverance.

ROMANS 8:25 NKJV

Waiting on you can be difficult, God, especially when I find that your timing is not mine. I know I need to practice perseverance and hope for what I do not yet see. I consider Moses, who led the Israelites into the desert for forty years before they could enter the Promised Land, and I can see that their idea of timing was not yours. They thought they would be living in plenty; instead they were faced with the scarcity of the desert.

But you didn't leave them. You were tangibly with them. You provided the food they needed to be nourished. As you were with them in their waiting, so you are with me in mine. You will not remove your presence from my life, nor will you cease to provide for the needs I have. I take hope as I persist in believing that you are leading me into your promises in your timing.

Faithful God, I confess that waiting has worn down my confidence. When I am discouraged, I will put my hope in you. You are faithfully with me and you will faithfully do what you have promised. You are the fulfillment of my soul's desire and I will press into you.

Stop Striving

Surrender your anxiety!
Be silent and stop your striving
and you will see that I am God.
I am the God above all the nations,
and I will be exalted throughout the whole earth.

PSALM 46:10 TPT

God, when I am caught in the cycle of stress and worry, it can feel like a cyclone, picking up speed with every anxious thought. It is my human nature to try to fix myself and my situation, but I cannot cultivate peace in the middle of chaos by tending to every scattered detail. You tell me to be still. You comfort me in my trouble.

Today, I surrender my anxiety to you. If it takes continually offering my worries to you as they pop up, so be it. This is not a one-time fix but a lifestyle of submission. When the swirl of anxiety begins, help me to take a moment, breathe deeply, and yield to you, my Maker. Let your peace wash over me as I surrender to you.

God of the nations, I yield my heart to you again today. Moment by moment, I lean into your grace that helps me to slow down when my fears begin to ramp up. You are kind and patient and you will never change. I breathe in your peace, letting it fill me up. Thank you for your provision in every moment.

Beautiful

You are altogether beautiful, my darling,
beautiful in every way.

SONG OF SONGS 4:7 NLT

There is nothing like being the object of someone's affection, Father. When I allow myself to be loved and adored without self-condemnation, my confidence is given the opportunity to grow. When I feel uncomfortable with this sort of love and attention, it reveals what I think about my own worth. Psalm 119 describes how you formed me in my mother's womb; you creatively knit me together with purpose and intention.

It is often hard for me to convince myself of how much you enjoy me. I know you don't create some people to be loved and others to endure unending rejection. Help me to understand that I was created with beauty and purpose, and I was made to be loved. I want to be encouraged by your devoted affection.

God, I admit that sometimes it is hard for me to believe that I am loveable as I am. Would you speak your words of life over me today and cause me to see myself from your perspective? I yield my self-protection and shame to you today. I don't want to be clouded by these things any longer. Show me who I am to you.

Always the Same

Jesus Christ is the same yesterday
and today and forever.

HEBREWS 13:3 NASB

When I consider your incredible life, Jesus, I can clearly see
the mercy, kindness, and love of the Father. Your Word says
that you remain the same yesterday, today, and forever.
Your character is constant. I don't have to wonder if you
will eventually become fed up with my weakness. You
spent the majority of your time on earth with those who
were broken and neglected by the world. In fact, the ones
you reprimanded were those who thought they had all the
answers and were using them to judge others.

Where I have felt less than, draw close to me. You comfort
the humble in heart. I want to let you into the deep places
of my soul. I know I cannot exhaust your compassion. Not
today, and not ever.

Jesus, I see now that you do not judge those who are weak
and struggling. Meet me in my weakness and strengthen
me with your gracious compassion. I won't hold back
myself from you today. I will reject the lie that my mess
is too much for you. I believe that you heal the wounded.
Heal me today, Lord.

April

You will call on me
and come and pray to me,
and I will listen to you.

JEREMIAH 29:12 NIV

Faith in Action

"Even more blessed are all
who hear the word of God
and put it into practice."

Luke 11:28 NLT

Father, my words only count for so much if they are not
backed up with action. Where I find myself in agreement
with your Word in what I say, think, or believe, may I be
one who lives these things out in practical ways. Let me be
someone who practices what I proclaim.

When I give others advice, help me to not only believe
what I am telling them but to also practice it myself. I don't
want to spout off answers because truth is just part of my
psyche. I want to make wise choices in my life and in my
relationships. I want to put my faith into action.

God, you are so incredibly gracious toward me. I ask for
eyes to see where my life is not aligned with your truth. By
your Spirit, help me to be empowered to live the truth of
your radical love in every area. You are worthy of my trust.

Conviction

Faith is the assurance of things hoped for,
the conviction of things not seen.

HEBREWS 11:1 ESV

God, thank you for the encouragement of Hebrews 11—the faith chapter. It recalls those who lived their lives tenaciously clinging to your promises, especially when those promises were far off and it was not clear how you would fulfill them. I have the hindsight of history that oversimplifies the process from promise to fulfillment.

They faced uncertainty and trials of many kinds although different than those I face. May I echo the faith they clung to, believing that you are the same God who came through for them and you will come through for me too. You are faithful to your Word and to your people. May my conviction in your goodness run deeper than the doubts that my shifting circumstances bring.

Holy One, you have been faithful through the ages. You have not changed your character; I take courage in the testimonies of those who have walked with you before me. There is nothing that separates me from your love, and certainly there is no circumstance that can derail your promises. Even as I cling to you, may my faith grow more secure.

Trust Him

You will keep in perfect peace
those whose minds are steadfast,
because they trust in you.

ISAIAH 26:3 NIV

Your loyal love has been proven over and over in the mercy you continuously extend toward me, God. Jesus embodied this better than any other example. His grace toward women, his friendship with the poor and broken, and his disdain for injustice, broke many cultural ideas of who you were. In the same way, you are unfaltering toward me with compassion. Help me to be firmly convinced that you will not change your view of me as your child.

It is natural for a child to trust their dependable, loving parent. I can have the same resolute trust in you, my good Father. There is an indescribable peace that comes with this kind of deep, reverent faith. May this peace be my portion today and every day.

Yahweh, you continually pour out your love on your children. You are my joy and my portion; fill me with your peace as I hold onto you. You are the one I cling to as if my very life depends on you because it does! You will not disappoint me. You will come through.

Wonderfully Made

I praise you because you made me
in an amazing and wonderful way.
What you have done is wonderful.
I know this very well.

PSALM 139:14 NCV

Creator God, when I look at the world around me, I see the diversity of beauty displayed before my eyes. You could have created one type of tree or one species of flower. Everyone could be living in the same climate with the same ecosystem. However, this is not the kind of world that you fashioned. In the same beautifully varied way that you created everything in nature, so you also created me uniquely.

Who I am is not accidental. You created me with purpose and with the personality and skills exclusive to me. I am beautifully and wonderfully made! Where I have unfavorably compared myself to others, help me today to see myself in all of my wonder. Reveal the greatness that you have put within me. Thank you that you delight in me.

My Creator, give me eyes to see myself the way you do. Remind me that I am fearfully and wonderfully made in your image. I ask that your words of life would pour over me today and that my heart would be open to receive your undiluted love. Tear down every wall that keeps me from this revelation.

Nourished by the Word

If you instruct the brethren in these things, you will be a good minister of Jesus Christ, nourished in the words of faith and of the good doctrine which you have carefully followed.

1 TIMOTHY 4:6 NKJV

Father, it is true that I become what I behold. What I spend my time consuming, how I fill my mind, and what I surround myself with feeds my soul. It is good and wise for me to stop and consider both the engaging, intentional sources and also that which becomes noise pollution.

Constant negative programming in the news, though real, does nothing to produce life and hope within my soul. It is the same in social media, the friends I spend time with, and so on. I want to be nourished by the goodness of your Word. I want to listen to things that uplift and challenge my heart. I want to surround myself with people who support me in love. When I am fed in these ways, I experience the life and health I long for.

Gracious God, I acknowledge that I have not been diligent about what my soul has been consuming. Wash my mind and my heart in your love, cleaning out the cobwebs of confusion. As I feast on your Word, fill my life with the fruit of your Spirit.

Compassionate Father

Praise be to the God and Father of our Lord Jesus Christ,
the Father of compassion and the God of all comfort.

2 CORINTHIANS 1:3 NIV

Father God, I don't want to view you as some far-off
grandfather figure who has arbitrary requirements of
me. You are not a being way off in space who demands
perfection. Your Word reveals you as a father and not some
absent father removed from the lives of your children. You
are the Father of compassion and God of all comfort.

When I consider this, how could I not be drawn to
you? You have more than enough understanding of my
circumstances. Your kindness and consideration are
beyond any that I could find in even my closest friend. You
are the God of all comfort. Not just some comfort. You
have more than enough reassurance to give, and you never
tire of consoling me.

Comforter, I easily forget the kindness and compassion
you have for me. Somehow, in the craze of life, I find
myself drifting from the conviction of your great love.
Today, I align myself with your character as a good father.
I remember who you have always been—the God of all
comfort. Surround me in the loving embrace of your
presence.

Strengthened by Love

May our Lord Jesus Christ himself and God our Father,
who loved us and by his grace gave us eternal comfort
and a wonderful hope, comfort you and strengthen you.

2 THESSALONIANS 2:16-17 NLT

God, when I find myself in the abyss of painful
circumstances, it can feel as though joy is lost forever.
There are some times in life where my experiences defy
the hope that I once held firm. When these dark seasons
drag on, I find it difficult to cope. How can I survive without
drowning in discouragement and despair?

You are called my comfort for a reason. You do not expect
me to be strong on my own merit. You draw close to the
humble, you are a friend to those the world looks down
upon, and you offer strength I could never conjure up. In
my weakness, in my pain, I come to you as a wounded
child. You are always there to offer the comfort I need.

Loving God, I come to you with my wounds and my pain.
Comfort me with your loving presence and wrap me in
your grace that strengthens me from the inside out. There
is no one who compares to you; what a wonderful Father I
have in you!

Never Worry

You will never worry about an attack
of demonic forces at night
nor have to fear a spirit of darkness
coming against you.

PSALM 91:5 TPT

When fear overtakes me, God, it can be debilitating. It is no accident that you say, "Do not fear" over eighty times in the Bible. You are my confidence and strength; you are a defender of the weak and a stronghold of security for the vulnerable. When I feel surrounded by darkness and impending doom, I turn my heart toward you.

You give peace to my restless heart and comfort me when I am grieving. You see every detail, and nothing I face is too difficult for you to turn around. You will never leave me; you are with me in every moment. I can trust you to take care of me.

Ever-present One, when I am tempted to give in to the overwhelming worries that lurk in the corners of my mind, I will turn to you in surrender. I have seen your faithfulness in my life, and I will trust you to continue to come through time and again. Thank you for your presence that is always with me.

How Long

How long must I worry and feel sad in my heart all day?
How long will my enemy win over me?

PSALM 13:2 NCV

Father, there are some seasons of life where I just can't see the light at the end of the tunnel. Grief, anxiety, and suffering are so familiar they have become my companions. And yet, when my heart feels like it can't take any more, your presence is still my portion.

It is not weakness to feel sadness, and it is not failure to need comfort and encouragement. God, be my comfort in the middle of my mess. Meet me where I am. I don't need to be anything other than who I am in this moment. All you require is my heart. In the midst of my longing, you are there.

Lord, here I am with my heart laid open before you. I believe that you see me and love me just as I am in this very moment. I am thankful for your love that never leaves me. Strengthen my heart to hold onto you today. Breathe hope into me again.

Perfect Faithfulness

L ord, you are my God;
I will exalt you and praise your name,
for in perfect faithfulness
you have done wonderful things,
things planned long ago.

I saiah 25:1 niv

When I consider your faithfulness, God, your track record is unmatched. You are trustworthy, and you always follow through with what you say. You are not fickle, and you never act out of anything but love. Your ways are so much higher than mine; you are so much better than I am. Your motives are pure and your heart is true.

Thank you for your kindness and reliability in my life. When I am having trouble pinpointing moments where you came through for me, I will look for evidence of your kindness all around me. I know I will find it.

Lord, you are my God. I know that you will continue to be faithful as you have always been. My heart takes hope in your great goodness today. You have done wonderful things, and I believe that I will continue to see your kindness displayed in my life.

Waiting on the Lord

Now, O Lᴏʀᴅ, what do I wait for?
My hope is in you.

Psᴀʟᴍ 39:7 ɴʀsᴠ

In the busyness of life, I have to practice slowing down, God. Waiting patiently has become a foreign concept. With you there is richness found in stillness. When I take a few (or more) moments to disconnect from the frenetic pace of my life, I find peace in the quiet.

Waiting is not always motionless, nor is it inactive. A posture of hope keeps me trusting in you and in your Word even as my timeline adjusts. When I am in places in between and I need to lean into love's pace, I have the opportunity to calibrate my heart with your perfect peace. It is always available and always in a measure of abundance.

Good Father, I trust that as I wait on you, you will fill me up with the perfect peace of your presence. You are full of compassion at every moment, and I lean into your care as I put all my hope in you. I trust you to do what you said you would do in your perfect timing.

Momentary Troubles

This light momentary affliction is preparing for us an eternal weight of glory beyond all comparison, as we look not to the things that are seen but to the things that are unseen. For the things that are seen are transient, but the things that are unseen are eternal.

2 CORINTHIANS 4:17-18 ESV

The troubles I face are only momentary in comparison with the eternal hope I hold onto, God. When this world has passed away and I am on the other side of eternity, the fulfillment of joy will be mine. There will be no more worry, no more tears of sadness. Your glory will be the light that never dims, and I will be fully alive.

Circumstances change. When I think through my last several years, none of them are identical. The things I worried about five years ago don't hold the same concern now. God, you are the same yesterday, today, and forever. What I am walking through today will not knock me out. I can get through this with you by my side.

Holy One, I set my eyes on you, the one who never changes. I have been so caught up in the shifting circumstances of my life, letting stress overwhelm me. Calm the anxiety in my heart. Today I fix my mind on you, my eternal hope and my joy.

Delivered from Darkness

He has rescued us from the kingdom of darkness
and transferred us into the Kingdom of his dear Son.

COLOSSIANS 1:13 NLT

God, you are light and all things are made alive in you.
When I align my life with yours, I find freedom to live
out your incredible love. I have been delivered from the
darkness that once covered and imprisoned me. I live in
your light even in the midst of my trouble and suffering. My
heart can dwell in perfect peace during the storms of life.

Where I have felt unseen and unheard, I take heart that
there is nothing hidden from your loving gaze. You can
and will meet me in the middle of my chaos and bring
the peace I desperately long for. I find my home in the
kingdom of love where there is a place for me. Darkness
cannot keep me away.

Deliverer, I have known your goodness in my life before, and
I believe that I will continue to see your faithful love poured
out. Thank you that I have a place in your kingdom of love
and that it can never be stolen! In your light I come alive.

Heart's Delight

Your laws are my treasure;
they are my heart's delight.

PSALM 119:11 NLT

When I am at a loss for what to do or where to turn, there is so much wisdom to be found in you, God. In your Word, I find instructions for life that breathe hope into my weary heart. When I submit to your ways, I am filled with everything I need.

Your ways are perfect, and you make no mistakes. When I am overwhelmed by the thought of tomorrow, it is easy to forget that your faithfulness displayed throughout the ages is the same faithfulness today. You will continue to be faithful in all of my tomorrows. I come to you to find my peace. You are my delight in every season.

God over all, you always offer grace when I need it. I am so aware of my need for you. Fill me with your presence that awakens my heart to hope in you. You have been faithful and you will always be. Lead me in your perfect wisdom and be my heart's delight.

Shining Light

"Let your light shine before others, that they may see your good deeds and glorify your Father in heaven."

MATTHEW 5:16 NIV

Lord, in the light of your presence, I shine. Just as the moon has no light of its own and yet it shines brightly at night, so I reflect your light. I do not depend on my own goodness, but yours, to stand out in my life. As I walk on the path of your love, I am changed into your likeness.

What a relief it is that I don't rely on my own strength. I am empowered to live as you did when I lean into your grace that is like an ever-flowing fountain, replenishing my thirsty soul. I press into your love today, hoping to reflect your heart as I live out of that place.

Father of light, you are the source of all life. I lean into your heart of love, knowing that as I receive out of the overflow of your heart, I have more than enough to give away to others. Thank you that your abundance is the measure I live out of, not my own scarcity. Be glorified in my life.

Lifelong Love

Surely your goodness and love
will be with me all my life,
and I will live in the house of the LORD forever.

PSALM 23:6 NCV

Father, you have never withheld your love from me. You are full of compassion, meeting me at every turn with kindness. This love that covers me in my triumphs and successes is the same love that carries me through our darkest days.

There is no moment, no season, and no circumstance where you have removed your presence from me. In you I find everything I need. All the days of my life are wrapped in your kindness. Where I have trouble seeing your perfect character toward me, help me recognize where you already worked things out for my good.

Loving Father, I am covered by your grace that empowers me to live with my hope set on you. Your presence is my portion today and forever. Fill me with your perfect love. If I am overwhelmed by anything today, may it be with your kindness!

God's People

The LORD will not abandon His people on account of
His great name, because the LORD has been pleased to
make you a people for Himself.

1 SAMUEL 12:22 NASB

Looking in your Word, God, I see evidence of your loyal
love. You don't give up or turn away from those who seek
you. And even if I turn away, you warmly and willingly
welcome me back! The prodigal son left his father's house,
going his own way, squandering his inheritance. When
he returned, he came as a broken man left with no other
options, covered in shame.

When he returned, the father didn't welcome him with a
cold shoulder or an, "I told you so." He ran to meet him
while he was still far away, covered him in his own robe,
and called for a celebration. The son was ready to beg to
live on his father's land as a servant, yet he was completely
restored as an honored son. In the same way, I will come
to you, God, with all of my shame and let you cover me in
your love, restoring me as your beloved child.

Gracious Father, you are full of mercy and kindness to all
who come to you. I will not stay away. I approach you with
the humility of my circumstances and the confidence of
your child. Even as I question how you could ever accept
me as I am, I freely come to you again. Wrap me in your
unfailing love.

Filled by Power

May the God of hope fill you with all joy and peace in believing, so that you may abound in hope by the power of the Holy Spirit.

ROMANS 15:13 NRSV

When doubts cause confusion to fill my mind, and hope feels like a lost luxury of the innocent, it is hard to find strength to persevere in belief, God. What then? Do I will change into existence? Do I punish myself because I have missed the mark yet again? Do I disqualify myself as not good enough?

God, you are not a taskmaster. You do not require perfection—not ever! You don't expect me to transform into a carbon copy of Jesus. I was created as a unique reflection of your love. It is the power of your Holy Spirit, my constant companion, that fills me with everything I need to live a life of faith, joy, peace, and hope. Where there is lack in my life, there is space for an invitation of your power to permeate and change me.

Holy Spirit, I invite you into my lack today. There is so much. Yet you are the hope that fills me and empowers me to persevere in believing for breakthrough. Bring peace to my mind and heart today. I welcome you to come and change me again from the inside out.

Pause in His Presence

As I thought of you I moaned,
"God, where are you?"
I'm overwhelmed with despair
as I wait for your help to arrive.
Pause in his presence.

PSALM 77:3 TPT

Father, there are times in life where there is no silver lining. I cannot create goodness out of what looks like desolation and destruction. It is not a failure to be desperate. When I can't see how anything can grow out of the devastation, I do not need to pretend to be hopeful.

In those moments, I come to you, asking you the questions that lurk in the corners of my mind. "Where are you" is often the cry that comes out. When all seems lost, help me to take the time to wait on you. This is an invitation to remember who you are. Not who you were or will be, but who you are right now. Yes, it's all the same because you are unchanging, but sometimes my heart needs the reminder that you are with me, right here and right now. I want to take a cue from the psalmist and pause in your presence.

Everlasting God, you are the same yesterday, today, and forever. As I come to you with the desperation of a heart that is overwhelmed, I take the time to pause before you. Come, Holy Spirit, and fill me with the power of your presence as I cry out for more of you.

Don't Fret

Be still in the presence of the LORD,
and wait patiently for him to act.
Don't worry about evil people
who prosper or fret about their wicked schemes.

PSALM 37:7 NLT

God, I cannot control what other people choose in this life. I can only command my own thoughts, heart, and life. With that in mind, how I choose to direct myself in the middle of chaos can determine the peace, or lack of it, within me.

Help me to still my thoughts and offer you my attention in the middle of the stresses and worry storms of my life. You are with me. As I cultivate a heart of surrender, choosing to direct my mind and heart toward you, you will fill me with the peace I long for. Your presence is always accessible. When I feel haste to act in my own defense, I will step back and let you, my protector, fight for me.

Defender, you are the one who keeps me in perfect peace while the storms of life rage around me. I still my heart before you today, offering you the space to speak your words of life over me again. I submit my mind to you. Fill me with the lifegiving stillness of your presence.

Freedom Now

The Lord is the Spirit,
and where the Spirit of the Lord is,
there is freedom.

2 CORINTHIANS 3:17 NIV

Where there is freedom, there is a feeling of open space—of opportunity, God. There is freedom to choose, freedom to live. When you created Adam and Eve in the garden, you gave them freedom from the beginning. You also gave instruction and wisdom. Friendship with you was the design, and it was their reality.

Jesus, friendship is still your design, and it is my reality in the freedom that you paid for with your very life. I don't need to wait for an unknown time and place to experience the original liberty of walking with you without anything standing in my way. I have your Spirit with me, and there is nothing that can separate me from your vast love.

Holy Spirit, you are the companion that encourages my soul and strengthens my heart to keep going in this life. I am so grateful for the freedom that you bring; it is always available and always more than enough. Bring fresh revelation of the liberty I have in you today!

New Life

There is hope for a tree, if it is cut down,
that it will sprout again,
and that its tender shoots will not cease.

JOB 14:7 NKJV

There is no situation so grim that you can't turn it around, Father. When I consider the life of Job, all the tragedies that he faced and the loss he dealt with, I am tempted to write off his experience as exceptional. As long as I am in this world, I will go through struggles and suffering. There's no doubt about it.

My hope is not anchored to my happiness or to shifting circumstances. My hope is secured in Jesus and in his resurrection. He overcame death—what then is left? My deepest fears are covered by your great love. I am safe and secure in you. You resurrect what was dead and bring new life to all you touch. I am yours, and you will surely revive me in your mercy, causing life to grow where I can only see barrenness.

God of all life, breathe hope into my heart again today. In you, even what was dead comes to life. You are the master reviver and rebuilder. I trust you to do the impossible in my life. Only you can.

Seen

Behold, the eye of the Lord is on those who fear him,
on those who hope in his steadfast love.

PSALM 33:18 ESV

God of the entire universe, you are the same God who knows every detail of my life. There is no aspect too insignificant that you overlook it. What matters to me, matters to you. You draw near even now covering me with your great love. I need not worry or run away—your compassion for me is greater than my fear.

What a wonderful King! Your love is more reliable than the rising and setting of the sun. I may take for granted that the stars will shine at night and that the tides will shift during the day, but your unfailing mercy is more constant than the most reliable workings of nature. Let us take hope in the loyal love of our Father.

Lord, I am reminded that my life does not go unnoticed by you. Comfort me as I look to you today. Bring resolution where I only see confusion and open-ended questions. Fill me with the confidence of your affection through the power of your presence. I need you.

I Will Praise

I will hope continually,
and will praise you yet more and more.

PSALM 71:14 NRSV

God, my hope is not in the mountains or the valleys I tread. It is not found in the circumstances of my life. My anticipation lies in the working out of your faithful character. You are slow to anger, abounding in love to all, you make all things new in your mercy—you are my great confidence. When my heart begins to waver, strengthen me by your nearness.

When I see evidence of your goodness, how can I keep from praising you? Why would I withhold my gratitude, overlooking instances of your mercy woven through my story? Help me to posture my heart to honor you. I want to offer you what I have and be filled with the wonder of a child as you meet me with your mercy and love me to life.

Faithful One, encourage my heart today in your loyal love. You never stop working. Give me eyes to see where you've planted your goodness in my life. My heart is open to you, Lord; come and have your way!

My Confidence

You are my hope; O Lord God,
You are my confidence from my youth.

PSALM 71:5 NASB

Children learn to value what is modeled. God, where I was taught the importance of self-reliance, I live as one who has to get things done on my own. Where I was taught the significance of honesty, I seek to tell the truth. Where I have learned to rely on you, I find that my heart trusts you as you faithfully lead me.

It is never too late for me to learn how to live submitted to your mercy and compassion. You are a restorer of all things even time! As I rely on you, I am changed into your likeness. My heart finds strength in your unfailing love, and your peace is my daily portion. You are more than able to make my life fruitful no matter how long it is. You are my true hope.

Lord God, you are amazing in your leadership. You bring healing and restoration to everything you touch. Come touch my life with your lifegiving presence again. You are my hope, and my greatest confidence is in you.

Restoration

"The blind see again, the crippled walk, lepers are cured, the deaf hear, the dead are raised back to life, and the poor and broken now hear of the hope of salvation!"

MATTHEW 11:5 TPT

What a wonderful God you are! You heal the sick, bring the dead to life, and save the destitute. These are not just nice ideas. Your power touches my life in tangible ways. If I struggle to see your goodness at times, I invite you to do what only you can do. You are the lifter of the broken; surely you will meet me.

There is no time limit to your mercy. Your promises do not have an expiration date. Today is the day of salvation. Today is the day I am given; it is all I have. I cry out from my heart straight to the heart of my good Father who always hears me. Where there are places of brokenness in my life, I know they can be touched by you.

Healer, I ask for you to restore me today. Touch my mind, my shattered spirit, and my body with your healing love. I cannot escape your grasp. Come near and revive me!

Delivered Again

He delivered us from such a deadly peril,
and he will deliver us.
On him we have set our hope
that he will deliver us again.

2 CORINTHIANS 1:10 ESV

God, your character never changes. You healed and you will heal again. You forgave and you will forgive again. You delivered your people and you will once again deliver them. You are better than I give you credit for. I cannot exhaust your all-encompassing mercy and compassion. My heart takes courage in the account that history tells of your goodness. That same goodness is mine.

When my hopes are set in your faithfulness, they will not be disappointed. Where I have struggled to hold onto optimism about my future and present circumstances, I yield my heart in surrender once again. When I stir up my history with you, I see with eyes of confidence, knowing that where you came through, you will come through again. You don't tire of helping me.

Good God, you are my constant help. When I remember your goodness displayed in my life, I can't help but be encouraged. May my heart find its confidence in your character not in the overwhelming worries of my present circumstances. You are so good!

Eager Expectation

It is my eager expectation and hope that I will not be put to shame in any way, but that by my speaking with all boldness, Christ will be exalted now as always in my body, whether by life or by death.

PHILIPPIANS 1:20 NRSV

God, my expectations don't find their fulfillment in my own strength or reliability. Even with excellence as my pattern, I falter. You are my covering, and you are perfect in all your ways. You will not let me be put to shame even as I walk through my pain and troubles.

My heart will find strength in your promises. With my eyes set on you, I will not be disappointed. You are my greatest reward. I can never reach the end of your lovingkindness, and I will never deplete your compassion. I will know and see you in all your glory when this life is over. Every hope I have pales in comparison to your grandeur.

Holy One, you are the expectation of my heart. Though I walk through the valley, I know that you are with me. I only see part of the picture, and you consider the whole. I trust you to guide me in your unfailing love all the days of my life. Be my strength and the joy of my life!

Cared For

Give all your worries to him,
because he cares about you.

1 PETER 5:7 NCV

When Jesus referred to you, God, he spoke of you as a
father. The relationship you had was one of closeness
and trust. Through the death and resurrection of Christ, I
was welcomed into the same connection. The good, kind,
faithful Father of Jesus is also my merciful, compassionate
Father.

I don't need to carry my worries around like obligatory
badges of adulthood. I am a child of yours with access
to your help at every moment. You never wanted me to
strive for survival on my own. When I am connected to you,
relying on you for the help I need, I find that worry is just
wasted energy. You can handle everything—I need only
trust you and follow your wisdom.

Father, you are the one I rely on in every situation. Here are
all of my worries and fears. You can have them all. I don't
want to sway from dread to hope like a pendulum. Be my
rock and firm foundation. You are my help, and you are
faithful. I lean into your support today.

Peaceful and Secure

"My people will live free from worry
in secure, quiet homes of peace."

ISAIAH 32:18 TPT

God, you are full of peace. You don't stir up dissension or cause conflicts. You are the great unifier. Though I live in a world full of chaos and reckless decisions, you are the opposite. You bring order and lead in perfect love and wisdom. As I bind myself to your goodness, I find the rest I long for in your presence.

There is no situation so messed up that you cannot bring redemption from it. You are the best at bringing stability to confusion. I am your child, called by your name. I have been adopted into your family. As your child, I am invited to live in the atmosphere of your good nature. Where you are, I can be confident of my safety. You keep and hold me. Help me not to lose heart or let fear overtake me.

God of peace, you are steady and sure. Your kindness is unmoving, your heart pure. With you, I know that I am covered. I don't need to worry about a thing. May my heart be filled with your peace today as I walk in your ways.

May

I pray that your hearts will be flooded
with light so that you can understand
the confident hope he has given
to those he called—his holy people
who are his rich and glorious inheritance.

EPHESIANS 1:18 NLT

No More Tears

God's dwelling place is now among the people, and he
will dwell with them. "He will wipe every tear from their
eyes. There will be no more death" or mourning or crying
or pain, for the old order of things has passed away.

REVELATION 21:3-4 NIV

As I wait for your kingdom to invade earth just as it is
in heaven, God, help my heart to find comfort and hope
in your presence with me here and now. Every painful
circumstance is temporary; suffering will not last forever.
Even as I endure the hardships of this life, your compassion
can cover me and carry me into the peace of your heart.

Though weeping may last for a season, I am not destined
for perpetual sadness. Even now I have you with me—
your presence is tangible through the Holy Spirit. You
strengthen me when I am weak, comfort me in my sorrow,
and help me in my need. Though the ultimate freedom
from pain is coming, I have a taste of this glorious reality
available through your nearness. You, my God and King,
are full of mercy.

Father, strengthen my heart to trust and my body to rest as
I take refuge in you. In my sorrow, I know that your comfort
is the only thing that can truly ease my agony. I lean on
your grace. Show up today in power.

Covered

You bless the righteous, O LORD;
you cover them with favor as with a shield.

PSALM 5:12 NRSV

God, sometimes when I share vulnerably, I feel really uncomfortable. When I feel exposed, you are closer than I know. You cover me. You bless the righteous, and all it takes for me to be considered righteous is to be submitted to you. You are a refuge for the weak, so I will find my rest in you.

When I feel weak, needy, and completely ill fitted, I trust that you will more than make up for what I lack. You do not expect me to have it all together. You don't require perfection. Your mercy meets me right where I am, and you cover me with your overwhelming love. I don't need to worry about a thing.

Lord, you are the hope of my heart. I am extremely aware of my own shortcomings, but all of it pales in comparison to your great love. Cover me today. Meet every need by your abounding grace. Your provision is better than any of my own plans.

Lifted Up

Humble yourselves in the sight of the Lord,
and He will lift you up.

JAMES 4:10 NKJV

God, you are close to the humble, and you lift up those who fall. When I think that I am too far gone, that is just when I find that your abundant mercy brings me back from the brink into love once again. You never give up, and you are not worried by the cares that overwhelm me.

I can never fall outside of your reach. You do not roll your eyes when you find I've wandered from your path of love again. You never leave me, and it is your nature to relentlessly love me to life over and over again. I couldn't exhaust your mercy even if I tried. Help me to find my home in your arms.

Loving God, your mercy knows no end. What a marvelous thought! Invade my life with your unfailing love that never lets go of me. Let your loyal heart encompass every failure, every shame, and every downfall in my life. I am nothing without you.

Continue Strong

Be alert. Continue strong in the faith.
Have courage, and be strong.
Do everything in love.

1 CORINTHIANS 16:13-14 NCV

When I look at your life on earth, Jesus, I find that everything you did in your ministry, you did out of love. You were the pure reflection of your Father. In your humility, you served those who should have served you. You laid down your life in love over and over again. You chose the way of peace, mercy, and kindness when confronted with trouble.

As I try to follow in your steps, love's example is my primary purpose. I find courage as I press into your presence. The strength to keep going is not found in my own motivation but in being filled by your great mercy every day. Your compassion never fails to satisfy me. Help me not to give up coming to you. Your abundance never wanes!

Merciful God, you are the source of everything I need. Even as I feel my strength and resolve weakening, I come to you. You are the giver of good gifts. Lead me in your love each new day. Guide me in your mercy.

Love Remains

Faith, hope, and love abide, these three;
but the greatest of these is love.

1 CORINTHIANS 13:13 ESV

Just when I think your love has become rote, you come in the power of your presence. Your presence changes everything. It goes beyond my logical understanding and brings peace where there was chaos. Your presence heals my mind and body. I cannot be touched by you and remain unchanged. I have not drained your resources, for you are the source of every good thing, and you never run dry.

Faith, hope, and love will always remain, and where they abide is where you are. I know that when my heart is full of these, you are alive in me, God. Where I lack them, I need only ask. You freely give to all who request. In your nearness, I find my heart comes alive in love.

Faithful One, you always show up in power. You don't grow tired or weary, dragging your feet. Your joy is abundant even as I barely glimpse at you. Come and let faith, hope, and love fill my heart. You are so good.

Renewed Strength

"You were tired out by the length of your road,
Yet you did not say, 'It is hopeless.'
You found renewed strength,
Therefore you did not faint."

ISAIAH 57:10 NASB

The road of life at times feels extremely short and unbearably long, Father. In seasons of suffering, I feel like there is no end to the pain and sorrow. Help me to remember that your character is absolutely unchanging. Though my circumstances shift, your mercy never does.

I will surely find my strength renewed along the way. As you remind me of your faithfulness, you continue to direct my path. Even as I stumble, you lift me up. As long as it is called today, there is hope. The journey of life is not over; defeat has not overcome me. I am led in love every day, with no exceptions!

God, you are my strength. When my resources run dry, I find that I have everything I need and more in your presence. Fill me today. Lead me on in your kindness. I lean on you as if my very life depends on it.

Freedom of Grace

Sin is no longer your master,
for you no longer live under the requirements of the law.
Instead, you live under the freedom of God's grace.

ROMANS 6:14 NLT

In the light of your love, I have been set free, God. I have been perfected in your Son, Jesus. I don't rely on my own abilities to do well or to perfectly perform. I am not bound by the strict confines of perfection—I would fail at it anyhow. Thank you for your mercy and grace that holds space for me when I fail. In my faltering, I am fully loved and known.

God, you do not turn away from the weak or the struggling. In fact, you draw near to the humble and refresh them with your comfort. Living under the freedom of your grace, I find that it is not so devastating when I mess up. There is mercy extended at every opportunity. I don't need to live in the shame of my mistakes; rather, I live within the liberty of your loyal love.

God, you are full of grace that never runs out. As I cling to you, I find love that lifts me out of every situation that weighs me down. You are so much better than anyone I've ever known. Purify me in your presence again today.

Submitted to Christ

My God, I want to do what you want.
Your teachings are in my heart.

PSALM 40:8 NCV

Jesus, your teachings are full of purpose. They reflect your good nature. Your perfect character is on display in your law of love. As I look to your instruction, I see that your ways are different than mine. Instead of seeking revenge, you humbly extended forgiveness to all. Instead of pursuing success and riches, you rejected them in favor of being close to the needy and broken. Instead of taking things by force, you peacefully offered your way as an option.

When I learn from you and put your law of love into practice, I find that the fruit is sweeter than any I have ever known. Your love satisfies in ways that no amount of worldly success could. Notoriety is fleeting, but a life of honor and purpose no one can take away. Help me submit my heart to your better way.

My God, you are the one I look to in my confusion. I trust you as I submit my life to you once again. I have to believe that you are making something good out of the situations I am walking through. With your help, I will walk in your way of love, finding fulfillment in your nearness and in the fruit of a life submitted to you.

Immeasurably More

To him who is able to do immeasurably more than all we ask or imagine, according to his power that is at work within us, to him be glory...for ever and ever! Amen.

EPHESIANS 3:20-21 NIV

In the midst of trial and change, when requests are ever on my mind, it sometimes feels like I am testing your patience, God. I continually ask for the overwhelming needs in my life to be met. But this isn't the case! You are full of patience, and you delight in me whenever I come to you. When I live in a posture of open relationship with you, both giving and receiving, I find that you are abundantly better than my wildest hopes.

Instead of holding back my questions and needs, God, today I want to lay it all out before you. It doesn't matter how many times I've asked; I will bring my requests to you again. You never tire of my voice; your power is at work within me. As I pour out my heart to you today, I will also take some time to receive your perspective and love for me. Your thoughts toward me are full of tender affection.

Holy One, you are the one I come to in every season of the soul. In times of need, I desperately come to you. Today again, I lay out my heart before you—every part! You see the obvious and the hidden spaces, so why would I try to pretend that they aren't there? Meet me, Lord.

Free from Anxiety

"Remain passionate and free from anxiety and the worries of this life. Then you will not be caught off guard by what happens."

LUKE 21:34 TPT

God, it takes practice to remain worry-free in this hectic world. When plans change and I need to adjust my expectations, it is easy to fall into the trap of despair and the swirl of anxiety. When I rely on my circumstances to find my happiness or my stability, I will be sorely disappointed.

Let today be the day I come to you, God, with all my cares—all my worries and anxieties. You can handle them, and I was never meant to bear them on my own. I will find the passion and freedom I'm looking for in you alone. I cannot carry myself through the storms of life and thrive. I choose to let go and lean into you today.

Savior, I rely on your strength to meet me in my weakness. I am not strong enough to get rid of the anxiety I feel. Instead, I come to you and ask that you would fill me with the power of your presence. Let your perfect love drive out every fear that keeps me stuck. Thank you, Lord!

Sanctuary

The LORD also will be a refuge for the oppressed,
a refuge in times of trouble.
Those who know Your name will put their trust in You;
for You, LORD, have not forsaken those who seek You.

PSALM 9:9-10 NKJV

God, you are a hiding place for those who need shelter
from the storms of life. You are a strong and sure
foundation, immovable. You are a wrap-around refuge,
impenetrable. How could I but put my trust in you when
you have proven yourself faithful over and over again?

You do not leave me to fend for myself when I come to
you. You do not abandon the heartsick and broken. You
tend to the wounded, healing them and caring for them.
You mend; you do not tear apart. Help me to run to you
in my time of need. You are full of hospitality and warmth
when I pursue you.

Protector, you have been my hiding place before, and I will
not hesitate to make my home in your love. Where I have
felt hesitant to approach you, I remember that you are
merciful. I come to you just as I am, broken state and all.
Heal me, Lord, as I rest in you.

Longing

My soul longs for your salvation;
I hope in your word.

PSALM 119:81 ESV

God, in the waiting, there is always longing. Sometimes aching, other times more wishful, the longing of the in-between is as real as the promise itself. The now and not yet is the tension of living with the hope of what is to come while experiencing a different reality. This can be discouraging if it is only the promise of something to come that I find fulfillment in.

Thankfully, in the waiting you are with me—Emmanuel. You never leave, and you have given us your life-giving presence, not only to sustain us but also to fill us with the abundance of your love. In the expectation of more to come, may I not lose sight of what I have right now.

Emmanuel, you are God with us. You are the hope of every longing heart, and I know that everything I need can be found in you. Even as I wait on your promises, I find joy in you, for in you is the fulfillment of every hope I have. Meet me here and now and remind me of your overwhelming goodness.

Free Indeed

> "If the Son sets you free,
> you are truly free."
>
> JOHN 8:36 NLT

God, you are not in the business of setting captives free only to enslave them to your purposes. I have been freed by your great love and mercy so that I am uncontrolled and uninhibited by fear. There are no catches in your love. You do not have a hidden agenda. Your love is pure and unblemished. You are not manipulative in love. You have always been about companionship.

As a lover of yours, God, I am free to follow you. I am free to choose how I will live. I am free. I want to live as one who has been liberated from dread and immorality? In the light of your love, I am able to see truth where before I was confused by lies. Your mercy is abundantly better than I can imagine.

Son of God, thank you for freedom. Where I have been bound up by fear and worried about taking a wrong step, flood my heart with your perfect love that brings with it the clarity of your wisdom.

Wisdom Found

Know that wisdom is thus for your soul;
If you find it, then there will be a future,
and your hope will not be cut off.

PROVERBS 24:14 NASB

When I search for wisdom, I can be sure I will find it in you, God. Why would I attempt to find it anywhere other than the source of wisdom itself? Your ways are not outdated, nor are they out of touch. Your ways are always the best, and your solutions are full of perfect understanding.

When I am lacking hope for my future, I lean into your presence, God. You are full of answers. Fill me to overflowing with your love that pushes back the fears that keep worries swirling around my head. Give me peace that brings clarity to every confusion. You are reliable. You will come through for me.

God of all wisdom, I need you to lead me into life. I have reached the end of my knowledge; I'm desperate to know what your solutions for my life are. Bring peace as I wait on you. With your love alive in my heart, I will confidently walk forward toward hope.

Encouraged to Hope

Whatever was written in former days was written for our instruction, so that by steadfastness and by the encouragement of the scriptures we might have hope.

ROMANS 15:4 NRSV

Looking through your Word, I find common themes that reveal your character, God. Your faithfulness is unquestionable when I consider how you always accomplish what you set out to do. Mercy triumphs over judgment every time. When people cried out to you throughout history, you consistently answered them. You still do.

Help me not to become weary in discouragement. God, you were with the Israelites, with David, with Ruth, with Paul, and you are the same God who is with me. You have not changed your mind about humanity—I am still the work of your hands and the object of affection within your heart. What encouragement I can find in remembering how you have come through for me in the past. You will come through again!

Faithful One, you are the God who never changes. In faithfulness is still how you operate. May my heart be encouraged as I walk in the way of the truth of your love as many have before me. Fill me with your hope.

Beauty from Within

Your beauty should come from within you—the beauty of a gentle and quiet spirit that will never be destroyed and is very precious to God.

1 PETER 3:4 NCV

Father, you do not judge me based on my outer appearance. You are much more concerned with the state of my heart than how put together I appear. A beggar with a heart of devotion and love is more beautiful than a shallow princess decked in the world's finest jewels.

My spirit is precious to you. Help me not to neglect the impact of my heart's attitude. When I keep my heart open in humility and submission to love, I cannot go wrong. I don't want to be discouraged when others overlook me; there is no need to compare myself to others. I am uniquely and wonderfully made, and I have infinite worth to you!

God my Maker, you know my heart better than even I do. Would you fill me with your love that keeps me soft and humble before you and others? I yield myself to you, knowing that beauty is much deeper than the skin. May the beauty of your work within me radiate from the inside out.

Saved by Faith

Believe on the Lord Jesus Christ,
and you will be saved,
you and your household.

ACTS 16:31 NKJV

When I believe in you, Jesus, it is more than just choosing in my mind to agree with what I've been told about you. I live aligned with your kingdom truth. I offer you my loyalty and commitment. I trust and rely on your goodness in my life even as I give myself to being united with your character.

Help me to determine where my loyalties lie as I consider how I live. Is the fruit of my life reflective of what I say I believe? Without judgment, I want to look objectively at what my life reveals as the things I am convinced of. Where there is discrepancy between what I say I believe and how I live, help me to find out why. I invite you into my processing. Show me the truth of your love over me, Lord.

Good God, in looking at my life, I see that there are holes and areas where I cannot see your goodness at work. There are pieces of me that are desperate and searching. I know that nothing is outside of your realm even the ugly parts of me that feel like too much. I yield my heart to you again. May my life be marked by loyalty to you and your love.

Without Hindrance

He proclaimed the kingdom of God
and taught about the Lord Jesus Christ—
with all boldness and without hindrance!

ACTS 28:31 NIV

When I look at the life of Paul, I find that he did not have it easy, God. When he was converted on the road to Damascus, he could not deny your life-changing power. Previously, he had tortured those who had claimed you as God. After this experience, he was forever changed. He devoted his life to preaching the truth of your powerful love all the days of his life.

Paul was imprisoned, mocked, and beaten over the course of his ministry. He did not consider that any of this meant he was living a life outside of your control—on the contrary! He considered the suffering he endured to be part of the cost of following you. He continually encouraged others not to be surprised by it but to count the cost as an honor. Suffering was not a hindrance to Paul's life and ministry. God, help me to be able to say the same.

God, you are gracious in your ways. When I don't understand the chaos of my circumstances, may I not let the whys distract me from whose I am. I belong to you, and I count everything as loss compared to knowing you. Fill me with your life-giving grace today.

Common Ground

When I am with those who are weak, I share their
weakness, for I want to bring the weak to Christ.
Yes, I try to find common ground with everyone,
doing everything I can to save some.

1 CORINTHIANS 9:22 NLT

There is a bond that develops in shared experience, Jesus.
Mutual understanding builds trust that allows me to open
to others in sincerity. You did not live as a recluse on this
earth or as someone who was out of reach. As the King
of Kings, you could have lived in riches, but that is not
what you chose. You humbled yourself, always welcoming
friendship with the lowest in society.

You were not exclusive in who you let approach you, so
I can feel free to come to you with all of my messes. You
have already seen it all. I have not been disqualified from
knowing and following you because of my weakness. You
welcome me in. In the same way, I show your love in my life
when I share in the experiences of those around me.

Humble King, you are incredible in the compassion you
exhibit to all who turn to you. There is no sin too great, no
darkness too overbearing, no sickness too beyond your
reach. In your kindness, may I find the grace to live your
embodied compassion toward myself and others. You are
so generous!

Saving Grace

My soul, why would you be depressed?
Why would you sink into despair?
Just keep hoping and waiting on God, your Savior.
For no matter what, I will still sing with praise,
for living before his face is my saving grace!

PSALM 42:5 TPT

When I am feeling low, it is hard to be motivated, Father. I find myself sinking into despair as I consider my circumstances. It is not failure to have a bad day or to feel overwhelmed; I don't need to feel shame about this.

At the same time, I have been given the gift of leadership over my mind and heart. When the troubles I face outweigh the hope I have, let me direct my soul's eyes back to you. You set the world in motion and you are still faithful. You are still working. You are still worthy. Today is an opportunity for me to praise you in the "not yet."

Savior, oh how I need you! You see the internal struggle I am faced with; as I choose to trust, hope, and wait on you, even when my soul is sinking, would you fill me with the encouragement I so desperately need? Thank you for your faithful presence. I know you will come through again. I praise you today.

Future Hope

Surely there is a future,
and your hope will not be cut off.

PROVERBS 23:18 ESV

The hope of the righteous is like a firmly rooted tree. No storm of life will tear me down because you, God, are my keeper. In areas of my life where I struggle to see any possibility that is not filled with destruction or despair, give me your perspective.

You are the restorer of all broken things; you specialize in bringing beauty out of the ashes of destruction. Where I see an end, you see a new beginning. You are constantly making all things new—even today, even in my life. I have not reached the end of your goodness; I have not tapped the limits of your mercy and grace. Surely there is a bright future for me as I walk through the pain of the present.

Good God, you are the one who turns my mourning into dancing. I know that I will see your goodness in my life again—I have to hold onto that hope. Fill me with your grace that empowers me. I yield my mind and heart to yours today. Fill me with the light of your presence.

Resurrection Life

Blessed be the God and Father of our Lord Jesus Christ,
who according to His great mercy has caused us to be
born again to a living hope through the resurrection of
Jesus Christ from the dead.

1 Peter 1:3 NASB

God, in your great mercy, you have always intended for me
to be alive in your love. In the communion of fellowship
with you, I find that you are full of compassion. Your
kindness is unmatched. When Jesus rose from the grave
and defeated death, it was with the same power that I have
through your Spirit.

Resurrection life is mine through you, Jesus. Just as you
were raised from death to life, so am I—both in eternity
and here in this life. You tore down every barrier that would
keep me from the abundance of your love. Where I see lack
in my life is an invitation to see your power at work. When
I align my life with you, I can be sure that you will turn my
mourning into gladness and my sorrow into joy!

Holy One, your mercy is beyond my understanding. Open
the eyes of my heart to see your power at work in my life
right here and now. Spirit, may you breathe your life into
my weary soul once again and wake me up. I honor you as
I cling to you.

Thoughts of Peace

"I know the thoughts that I think toward you,"
says the LORD,
"thoughts of peace and not of evil,
to give you a future and a hope."

JEREMIAH 29:11 NKJV

God, your ways are better than my ways and your thoughts are above mine. Your intentions toward me are good—full of peace and kindness. You do not wish me harm, and you do not plan my destruction.

When my thoughts are not filled with peace about my circumstances or about myself, I can rest assured that they are not your thoughts toward me. I may be feeling the chaos of worry about the future, but you are not worried. Your plans always include mercy, love, and hope. When I am struggling to feel hope for my future, I ask for your perspective of my life.

Lord, your Word says that your thoughts toward me are full of peace. I ask for fresh revelation today to know the clear difference between your voice and my own. You are always better than I am, so I trust you to help me and breathe hope into me again. Thank you for your endless kindness, Lord.

Great Confidence

He's the hope that holds me
and the Stronghold to shelter me,
the only God for me,
and my great confidence.

PSALM 91:2 TPT

Father God, there is not much in this life that is absolutely stable. Economies fluctuate, families break apart, and the weather is increasingly unpredictable. What I can be sure of is that though changes happen outside of my control, you are always a shelter to take refuge in. You never change; you are not like the shifting winds.

When I feel the weight of uncertainty threatening my peace, I remember that you are the hope that holds me. Everything else is but a detail, and you are more detail oriented than I could ever be. Be the safe place where I run; I find my confidence in your incomparable goodness. You will not let me down.

God, you are my greatest treasure. Everything I could ever need and more is found in you. Where my mind has been swirling from the unknown and stresses of life, breathe your peace. You're the only God for me. May I be full of confidence when I consider your greatness.

Answered

By awesome deeds you answer us with deliverance,
O God of our salvation;
you are the hope of all the ends of the earth
and of the farthest seas.

PSALM 65:5 NRSV

I cannot escape the shadows of this world, where trials come in many different forms. I may be faced with sickness, depression, grief, or failure, but that is not my end. God, you are the hope of all the ends of the earth; you are my hope.

Just as you delivered the Israelites out of the hand of Egypt, so will you deliver me. Whatever dark season I am walking through is not the end of my story. You will come through for me and lead me into freedom again. The sun will rise, and your light will make all that is hidden clear as day. I wait for you. You will answer me.

Yahweh, you are my salvation. I believe that you have not abandoned me to the darkness of my circumstances. Shine your light on my life and lead me into your joy! I lift my eyes to you again, Lord, my hope and my deliverer.

Guided by Truth

Guide me in your truth and teach me,
for you are God my Savior,
and my hope is in you all day long.

PSALM 25:5 NIV

God, you are not a tyrant, and you are not demanding. You are an amazing leader and the best teacher I could ever find. The Holy Spirit is my constant companion, leading me into all truth. What an amazing gift you have given me in your presence that is always with me. What incredible hope that you have given me instructions in your Word that guides me.

When I look at the way of love, which is the way that you lead, I can be encouraged that everything I am learning and doing in this life is covered by grace. I don't need to get it right to be righteous—you have already done that work for me. There is room in your love to make mistakes as I learn to walk in your way. As I keep my heart humble before you, I am able to keep growing as your child.

Lord, you are so gracious in the way you lead. Help me to remember that you correct with kindness and you direct with love. I want to be just like you. I know that your way is better than my own. Guide me, God; you are where all my hope lies.

Believe

To all who did accept him and believe in him
he gave the right to become children of God.

JOHN 1:12 NCV

The eyes of faith help me cling to what is beyond my natural vision. God, you are not a man that you should lie, nor do your intentions change. As you were at the beginning, so you will always be. Where I have a wrong understanding of your character and nature, may my heart be molded by the love that meets me in my humility.

Belief is not a blind action, ignoring the reality around me. I can believe in you and also bring you every question, every wondering, and every hesitation. As your child, I have the relationship of family to approach you with every shallow and deep thought. You lead me, nurture me, and correct me in kindness. How could I be unchanged by such an exchange?

Father, I come to you today as a dearly loved child, knowing I do not need to hold anything back from you. In vulnerability, I approach you with my longings, questions, and my devotion. Knowing I am loved and accepted by you fills my heart with the confidence that with you I can face anything.

Not Afraid

"This is my command—
be strong and courageous!
Do not be afraid or discouraged.
For the LORD your God is with you
wherever you go."

JOSHUA 1:9 NLT

There is no doubt that I will face many tests in this life. There is no way to avoid trials and troubles though they look different for everyone. God, you are with me in whatever circumstance arises. There is nothing too difficult for you, and you will never look at me, or my situations, and decide it is too much for you to be invested in.

There is a reason that your Word encourages me to be strong and courageous. What does courage look like? In the face of fear, it is perseverance. In the face of discouragement, it is refusing to give up hope, even if it feels like the smallest sliver. Help me to join with those who have gone before me, fighting the good fight, keeping the faith, and finishing the race.

Lord my God, I take courage in your Word that says you are with me wherever I go. When fear threatens to immobilize me, I will abide in you, allowing your presence to empower me with what I cannot conjure up on my own. You are life to my soul, breath to my lungs, and refreshing water that washes over me. You are my God, and I am yours!

Eyes Opened

I pray that the eyes of your heart may be enlightened, so that you will know what is the hope of His calling, what are the riches of the glory of His inheritance in the saints.

EPHESIANS 1:18 NASB

God, I've had those lightbulb moments. Those profound instances where I understood something that was previously hidden from me. This is what revelation is. I consider when I first believed that Jesus was your Son. I was so captivated by him.

There is no end to the revelations of your character in my life. There is always more. You are infinitely better than I could ever imagine you to be. Today, may the prayer of Paul to the Ephesians pave the way for the eyes of my heart to be enlightened by the glorious reality of your goodness. You are full of unending wonders to discover!

Glorious King, illuminate the eyes of my heart to see the wonder of who you are in a new way today. May I see clearly the way you physically provide for your children. May my imagination be filled with the glory of your light alive in me. You are so good, Lord!

Real Revelation

Your faith and love rise within you as you access all the treasures of your inheritance stored up in the heavenly realm. For the revelation of the true gospel is as real today as the day you first heard of our glorious hope, now that you have believed in the truth of the gospel.

COLOSSIANS 1:5 TPT

There is a rich beauty in understanding the gospel, God, the fruit of which is that souls are won over by your love. There is freedom to come alive in the affection that has led me back to your arms.

I am not bound by duty; you are not a slave driver, requiring more of me than I can give and working me to the bone. You are a loving leader who calls me to a better way—the path of love. You showed us the way to live, love, and lead in the way you poured out your own life. You don't require perfection from me; you take my willing, open heart and as I live out love, I find that I am continually filled with more, straight from your heart. Let my faith arise today.

Glorious God, thank you for the mystery of the gospel that fills me with hope to live out of the generosity of your heart. Truly everything you do is done out of deep affection. Where there is resistance to this within my heart, I ask for fresh revelation to receive your abundant love. May faith arise within me today.

Anchor of the Soul

This hope we have as an anchor of the soul,
both sure and steadfast,
and which enters the Presence behind the veil.

HEBREWS 6:19 NKJV

Through your faithfulness, God, to your Word and intentions, my soul has been anchored to the King of heaven and earth. My hope is not dependent on myself or my own feeble belief. My hope is sure, never shaken, because it is based on your loyalty, Holy One who never fails.

This anchor of my soul keeps me from drifting with the shifting tides and winds. Even when storms come, I will be held secure. May my heart find confidence in you who holds me steady. You are faithful to do everything that you set out to do. When I struggle to see purpose in my life and can't see how things will ever work together, help me to remember that even when I cannot see, you know the bigger picture and you are not done with me yet!

Holy One, you are faithful. You keep me firmly planted in your love. Thank you for never letting go of me no matter what happens in this life. I trust you even as confusion crops up. You are better than I am, and I know that I will see your hand of mercy on every area of my life.

June

"Whatever you ask in prayer,
believe that you have received it,
and it will be yours."

MARK 11:24 ESV

Endurance

Love bears all things,
believes all things,
hopes all things,
endures all things.

1 CORINTHIANS 13:7 ESV

Your very character is love, God. Jesus bore and endured everything that came his way. He believed and hoped through every circumstance. When I do the same, I am reflecting your nature. You are alive in me. You are able to do immeasurably more than I could ever ask or imagine. Why would I not trust you?

As I endure the hard circumstances of life, your grace strengthens us. I am not left to do any of it on my own. I have access to the same Spirit who empowered Jesus to rise from the grave! Because death truly was defeated, anything I face is certainly covered by the same overcoming power. I will hold on to you; you are not done with me yet.

Compassionate One, you are the one I hold onto throughout my life. I cannot let you go, and even if I did, you would not let go of me. Fill me with your tangible love that strengthens and empowers me to live as Jesus did. You are worth it all!

Heartsick

Hope deferred makes the heart sick,
But desire fulfilled is a tree of life.

PROVERBS 13:12 NASB

Longings of the heart are not small matters to you, God.
When promises are delayed and I am waiting, it can
be hard to keep believing in hope. My heart breaks as I
struggle with disappointment. But you are not cruel. Even
as I wait, you are present with me in the heartbreak and
the longing.

As I wait on my delayed desires, I find my comfort in your
arms, my loving God. You are no consolation prize—you are
the ultimate goal. You are better than the gifts I am waiting
on. They reveal your character; they are glimpses of the
enormity of your goodness and glory. I know you are with
me, and you are the fulfillment of every longing I have.

Lord over all, you are the answer to every longing. What I
think is good is just a glimpse of something even better—
you! Fill my heart with hunger for fellowship with you as
you reveal yourself through the gifts you give. I know that
you are really what I long for.

Steadfast Hope

The LORD takes pleasure in those who fear him,
in those who hope in his steadfast love.

PSALM 147:11 NRSV

God, your love is steadier than the largest mountain on earth. You will not be swayed away from compassion or mercy—it is who you are. In the same way, I find hope in your unending, unmoving, fiery love. When all seems lost, help me to lift my eyes to you. You never change your mind about me.

Hope does not always come easily; it is like warfare to anticipate your goodness in the face of trials and circumstances that test my belief systems. When it comes down to it, my confidence is not based on my own works or worth; it is based on you. I take hope in you today.

Lord, you are where all my hopes find their fulfillment. You are the hand that steadies me throughout my life. Help me to stay close to you. I am yours for all my days. Meet me in the middle of my mess, Lord, and fill my heart with your peace.

Hurry to Help

God, hurry to help me, run to my rescue!
For you're my Savior and my only hope!

PSALM 38:22 TPT

There are times in life that I am desperate for your intervention, Father. There is no other way to describe my need than absolute dependency on a miracle maker. When I am solely reliant on your involvement to change my situation, it can feel like I'm grasping at the air. But this is not the case.

You are a rescuer, an ever-present help in times of trouble. I cry out to you from the depths of my soul and watch as you come to my aid. You will do it because you are faithful. You are the God of angel armies and you will save me. I wait on you, knowing that you will not delay.

Savior, I need your help more than I can express. When my heart starts to quake with fear, I turn to you. Hear me and save me! You are the solid support I need and my only hope.

Yes and Amen

All of God's promises have been fulfilled in Christ
with a resounding "Yes!"

2 CORINTHIANS 1:20 NLT

Your promises, God, do not depend on my ability to accomplish them. They belong to you and they are sealed by your faithfulness. Though I falter in faith, you never waver in dependability. You are the same yesterday, today, and forever. All of your ways are just and true. Though the seasons shift and everything changes, you are the steady foundation, my unshakeable hope, who never ever varies.

Where I have felt my hope start to fade, I press into your character. I remember my history with you, and I am reminded of your loyal love. You don't change your mind. I am yours, surrounded by your peace and full of your mercy. I reach out to you again today. I will not be disappointed in your presence.

Faithful One, your loyal love is the sustenance of my soul. When I am depleted of hope and any strength to keep going, I know that you are more than enough for me. Holy Spirit, fill me as I wait on you. Encourage my heart today in your kindness.

Brave Enough

On the day I called you,
you answered me.
You made me strong and brave.

PSALM 138:3 NCV

God, you are always ready to answer my cries when I call out to you. You do not delay. You don't try to prove a point in silence or feed my insecurity by making me wait. Even in the waiting, I find that the fullness of your presence is my portion. You do not give sparingly; you always offer the abundance of your heart.

When circumstances have me unsure of the outcome, I can find my rest and security in your character. I find courage in the loyal love of a good and faithful Father. In you, I find the strength I need. You will not fail me, and you will not betray me. Your nature is always compassionate, merciful, and generous.

Steady One, you are the rock I stand upon. Today, I call on you, and I trust that you will answer me. Meet me with the power of your presence. In my weakness, be my strength and encourage my heart. You make me brave.

Wonderful Things

LORD, you are my God;
I will exalt you and praise your name,
for in perfect faithfulness
you have done wonderful things,
things planned long ago.

ISAIAH 25:1 NIV

God, your ways are full of wisdom. You see the big picture as well as every detail. You are not reckless in the ways you move, and you are not distant. You work in perfect faithfulness, always following through. You do not forget your promises, and you do not grow weary of fulfilling any of them.

Where I struggle to see your goodness in my life, help me to look to your character. Have you forgotten anything? Have you left any detail untouched? In your mercy, you meet me right where I am, but you do not leave me there. You pick me up and lead me on in your perfect love. Help my heart to take hope in your faithfulness.

Lord, you are my God. You are the one I depend on in every circumstance. In your perfect faithfulness, meet me and fulfill every one of your promises in wonderful ways. You are so, so good!

Wait on the Lord

It is good that one should hope
and wait quietly for the salvation of the LORD.

LAMENTATIONS 3:26 NKJV

When the chaos of my life won't relent and the anxieties
in my mind prevent me from resting, help me to take time
to quiet my heart in your presence, God. Sometimes this
looks like intentionally crying out to you for help; other
times, it is taking a few minutes in a quiet place to breathe
deeply and slowly.

Your salvation is always at hand. You do not abandon
me to the overwhelming despair that comes from
uncontrollable situations. When sorrow, pain, and suffering
are unavoidable, you show up in the power of your
presence to sustain, comfort, and carry me. You are my
best and truest hope. In you, nothing goes wasted. Not
even the darkest night. In the waiting, you are there.

Loyal God, you consistently show up to save me. You are not
a one-time help in times of trouble—you are always available,
and you never hesitate to show up. I need you today. Calm
the anxieties of my heart as I look to you. Meet me with the
power of your presence, bringing peace to the chaos.

Do Not Forget

You have forgotten that Yahweh, your Maker, stretched out the skies and laid earth's firm foundation. But you live each day constantly worrying, living in fear of your angry oppressor who is bent on your destruction. But their fury cannot touch you!

ISAIAH 51:13 TPT

God, sometimes I am not entirely convinced that you will keep me safe. When I feel defeated and overcome by failure or overwhelming circumstances outside of my control, sometimes I succumb to worry. I often forget to turn my heart immediately in trust to you, my defender and Savior. Your power has not diminished over time and your heart of love has not changed.

Maker of heaven and earth, you are my Father. You do not abandon me to destruction. In your faithful love, you protect and guide me. You are my deliverer. You will not feed me to the wolves or let me be overcome by those who seek to humiliate me. You are so much better than that. I am hidden in your love, and you will sustain me through every trying circumstance.

Yahweh, you are all powerful. Your love is the strongest force in the universe, and I am completely covered in it. I will take hope in you again today, turning my eyes to you every time I am overcome by the worries of life. You are above them all and you are faithful to deliver me.

Provision Is Yours

"Do not worry then, saying,
'What will we eat?'
or 'What will we drink?'
or 'What will we wear for clothing?'"

MATTHEW 6:31 NASB

In you, God, I have access to everything I need. When I don't know how I will get by or get through, you miraculously provide for me. You are not slow to save or delayed in your response to me. When the Israelites wandered the desert before entering the Promised Land, they were fed straight from heaven each morning. The manna they received was incredibly provided, and they didn't even need to ask.

In the same way, I can trust that you will supply everything I need. I don't need to beg you to give me what I need to survive. You do it out of the goodness of your faithful heart. Your track record of provision is perfect. Why do I even worry about the essentials of my life being met? It is all delivered from your abundant storehouse. You always have more than enough. I will not go without.

Provider, I remember again today that everything I need is offered from your generous heart. I will not go without the sustenance I need; worry is just wasted effort. Fill me with the peace and confidence that comes from your nearness. You are everything I need.

Always Gracious

The LORD always keeps his promises;
he is gracious in all he does.

PSALM 145:13 NLT

When I consider your faithfulness, God, there is no room to doubt your goodness toward me. Even if I do, it does not affect your loyalty. I cannot jinx your mercy; I cannot affect your integrity. You stand alone in compassion, always giving it out of your generous heart.

You don't go back on your Word, and I cannot talk you out of your intentions. In everything you do, you are full of mercy. Your grace is given freely in every circumstance, fueling me with strength. Where I lack, you have more than enough. You are benevolent and kind, always considerate and gentle in the way you deal with me. I don't need to fear punishment or retribution in your presence. As I experience your caring, I grow more confident.

Gracious God, I can't begin to thank you for your generosity toward me. You never fail to reach out in love, and you don't leave me dry. Your mercy is my life-blood—it strengthens me. I rely on you today. You are faithful.

Safe Place

The LORD is good,
a refuge in times of trouble.
He cares for those who trust in him.

NAHUM 1:7 NIV

All those who come to you for shelter from the storms of life will find rest in your arms, God. You are a caring Father who always supplies what I need. Your comfort is unmatched; it's even better than the most empathetic mother in the world. Your character is good, and you will never let me down.

When I consider trusting you with the outcomes of situations in my life, sometimes I find comfort in you being in control. At other times it stirs up even more anxiety. Where there are doubts about your goodness, I bring them to your feet. Let's talk about this, God. You can handle every question I have. I want to lay everything bare before you without holding back.

Lord, here I am with all of my questions and my doubts. Here I am with my feeble trust. I want to know the confidence of faith in your good character. I believe that you are my best option even when I struggle to hope in your love. Holy Spirit, override my mind with your perfect peace. Encounter me with your presence today.

Fully Equipped

All scripture is inspired by God and is useful for teaching, for reproof, for correction, and for training in righteousness, so that everyone who belongs to God may be proficient, equipped for every good work.

2 TIMOTHY 3:16-17 NRSV

Where I lack trust in you, God, there must be a gap in my understanding of your perfect nature. I can find everything I need—every resource and all the strength I require—within your presence. In your Word, I find keys to living a life that is full of the fruit of your Spirit. As I yield myself to you, I submit my heart to your wisdom and follow in the path of love you have paved for me.

Where I have need, you have provision. Where I have questions, you hold answers and solutions. You are so much better than the best teacher. There is no problem that can confound you. There is no mountain that you cannot move. You are perfect in power, in wisdom, and in compassion. There is none like you.

Good God, I am so indebted to your faithfulness. Where I have struggled to see your love at work in my life, open my eyes to your perspective. Even as I struggle, I hold onto hope that you really are all I need. Come through for me, Lord!

Listen Closely

My child, pay attention to my words;
listen closely to what I say.
Don't ever forget my words;
keep them always in mind.

PROVERBS 4:20-21 NCV

In the craziness of life, slowing down and paying attention to details can seem overwhelming. When you speak, God, you do so in the gentle whisper of love and mercy. You are kind, and often it is kindness that I overlook. When someone acts uncharacteristically generous, it fills me with wonder.

For you, generosity is your signature. You are full of compassion to all who come to you. If someone is claiming to speak on your behalf, and what they're saying is not laced with love, help me to question the source. When I consider your unchanging character, I can listen closely for your whisper in my life and find that you are there. You are present with me. Your love never lets go!

Father God, you are the author of mercy, full of lovingkindness. When I look in your Word, I find that you continually met people with the goodness of your character. Knowing that you don't change, I am full of hope that you will also meet me with the kindness of your presence! Reveal yourself in a new way today, Lord.

Rightful Pursuit

Whoever pursues righteousness and love
finds life, prosperity and honor.

PROVERBS 21:21 NIV

You are light, and in you everything is brought to light,
God. You make the most muddled situations clear with the
precision of your perspective. As I pursue your good nature
in my life, I find the life and honor I am looking for. I will find
all the fullness I seek in your virtues as God and King.

As I worship you, I begin to understand that you are better
than any expression of love I encounter on this earth. You
are purer than my highest morals. You have no hidden
motives, and as I am filled by your revelation light, I find
that I need not. My loving response to living submitted to
your heart is a natural response to the unfiltered worth I
find in being loved by you, the King of kings.

Merciful King, you are above all and yet you are concerned
with every little detail. Nothing escapes your notice,
least of all me! As you fill me with the liquid love of your
presence, I am empowered to love you and others in
return. Your ways are so much better than any I've ever
known. Thank you for life.

Hiding Place

You are my hiding place;
You shall preserve me from trouble;
You shall surround me with songs of deliverance.

PSALM 32:7 NKJV

When troubles overtake me and I am overwhelmed by the demands of life, help me to turn to you, Father. You are a safe place to find refuge. You never turn me away when I look to you. You keep me secure in the covering of your love. I can never go outside of the confines of your kindness and compassion.

When I feel exposed by my fear, God, shield me in your great affection. You cannot be convinced out of your mercy. It isn't within the realm of possibility because you are love. When I feel completely out of my depth, I can be sure that you are never overwhelmed. You are full of wisdom when I need it. Your love never fails!

God, you are my hiding place. I run to you in my fear—when I am overwhelmed, you come in with your perfect peace and cover me. I don't want to venture out on my own; I rely on you today and every day.

My Only Hope

It is through him that you now believe in God, who raised him from the dead and glorified him, so that you would fasten your faith and hope in God alone.

1 PETER 1:21 TPT

Jesus, you are the purest example of the Father's love. You embodied relationship with the Father and the expression of his compassion to all. It is through you that I am given access to the same kind of close relationship with my good Father who never fails and is perfect in his parenting. I need never fear hidden motives lurking within your heart because you are pure, transparent love.

When my expectations in life are disappointed and my plans fall apart, I admit I am often shaken. I know failure is inevitable, and setbacks are par for the course. There is no perfect life. Your mercy is full of amazing fruit. You take the ashes of my circumstances and make something sweet grow out of them. Your plans are better than any I could make. As I stay connected to you, I find that you orchestrate a beautiful medley out of what sounds strange in isolation. You are blending the pieces my life together even now.

God, you are my hope. Take my life and make it something beautiful. I trust you to lead me into life; you are so good.

United Heart

Teach me your way, O Lord,
that I may walk in your truth;
unite my heart to fear your name.

PSALM 86:11 ESV

Where my heart is divided, there is competition for control.
When I follow you, Lord, walking in your truth, I submit
my heart wholly to you. I lead myself into your presence
and you lead me into life. There is no better guide in this
existence. You are the author of time and space, and you
direct my steps.

Is my heart completely yours? Help me to allow you into
all of me. I know there are parts of me that distrust even
you, God, so I invite your Spirit to minister wholeness to
every part of my being. As I welcome your presence to
bring restoration and change in me, I submit myself to your
goodness. You are tender and kind.

Lord, you are the kindest healer there is. You mend
with compassion. How could I not trust your goodness?
Especially where I struggle, you are welcome to speak your
words of restoration life. You are better than I am, and I
know I can rely on you to make me whole.

In the Meantime

Training us to...live lives that are self-controlled, upright, and godly, while we wait for the blessed hope and the manifestation of the glory of our great God and Savior, Jesus Christ.

TITUS 2:12-13 NRSV

In this life, waiting is a given. Patience is not. Endurance is conditioned with intentionality and practice. As I yield to your ways, I am constantly being trained in your character. I get to train in your nature so I reflect you. You are full of wisdom that is clear minded. You are righteous in all your ways; your intentions and actions do not change based on different people or locales. You are pure in love, never withholding compassion from me when I seek you.

I want to bear the fruit of your kingdom as I practice being peaceful and kind. As I forgive those whom others hate, I exhibit your mercy. When I choose to meet others in their suffering, I practice the same kind of comfort I receive from you.

God, I want to live a life that reflects your amazing character—full of compassion, kindness, tender mercy, and wisdom. It is not a chore to be loved by you, and though it is not easy to live that same kind of love, it is so worth it to choose it!

Run to Safety

The name of the Lord is a strong tower;
the righteous runs into it and is safe.

PROVERBS 18:10 NASB

There is so much that threatens my peace throughout the day, God. Whether it's physical, spiritual, or emotional, I face crises that drain my strength and resources. I only have so much to give, and when it's gone, what then? When I am depleted of my own means to get by, help me to run into your shelter.

Where you are, there is hope. You cover me with compassion as I run to you. You are my place of safety and refuge; you are not intimidated by the struggles I face. When arrows fly toward me, you wrap around me, and the arrows are absorbed by your tender mercy. You will not let me fall, and you won't let me be overtaken. You are faithful!

Lord, you are the place I find reprieve and rest from the storms of life. I look for comfort around me, but I only find true consolation in you. May the power of your presence surround me as I run toward you. Be my shield and my defender.

All I Need

The LORD is all I need.
He takes care of me.
My share in life has been pleasant;
my part has been beautiful.

PSALM 16:5-6 NCV

Father, when I feel isolated and alone, everything seems harder. I was not meant to carry myself through life by sheer willpower. I need help, and I require community to thrive. Leaning on others in my weakness is not a fault; it is a strength!

When I have no one around me who understands what I am going through, especially in suffering, the weight of pain can feel especially heavy. But you understand, God. You are my comforter, and you are with me in the most soul-crushing agony. You do not write off my suffering, but you meet me in the middle of it with your mercy and power. You take care of me and turn my ashes into beauty every time.

Lord, you are all I need. When I feel alone in my sadness, meet me in the middle of it with your unfailing love. Strengthen me and hold me up. I am so grateful that you take care of me perfectly. Surround me with your presence and put people as supports in my life as well.

Generous Living

"Give, and it will be given to you. A good measure, pressed down, shaken together and running over, will be poured into your lap. For with the measure you use, it will be measured to you."

LUKE 6:38 NIV

Your heart, God, is abundant in nature. It cannot be held in; it would surely burst at the seams if I attempted to contain it. When I live with generosity as a value, I reflect your character. Not only that, but when I give out of the willingness of my heart, I will be filled in the same measure.

There is no lack in your heart, and I don't need to worry about exhausting your resources. With access to the source of all life, I can freely live out the same generosity that is liberally given to me with no concern of running out. Where I have need, I can be sure that you will meet it. I don't have to be anxious about your provision.

Gracious God, you generously give to all who come to you. As you fill my life with everything I need, may I in turn be liberal in love to those around me. Give me confidence as I rest in your presence.

Never Disappointed

Here's what I've learned through it all:
Don't give up; don't be impatient;
be entwined as one with the Lord.
Be brave and courageous, and never lose hope.
Yes, keep on waiting—for he will never disappoint you!

PSALM 27:14 TPT

My timing is not the same as yours, God. When I am waiting, it can feel discouraging when I am doing it on my own with no end in sight. But when I actively connect with you in the delay, I find that your faithful character sustains me. You are my source of courage—not my own tenacity.

When I am tempted to give up, help me not to let go of hope altogether. As I remain knit into your presence, I find grace to continue to wait. Though circumstances may disappoint, you never will. Your nature is faithfulness, and I can rely on your goodness to be present every step of the journey.

Faithful One, you never let me go. Even as I falter in faith, you hold on tight. Give me courage to continue to press into you in the waiting and to trust that you will never go back on your promises. You are so good, God!

Coming Joy

The hope of the righteous ends in gladness,
but the expectation of the wicked comes to nothing.

PROVERBS 10:28 NRSV

It is a good, if painful, practice to exercise awareness of where my expectations lie, Father. What do I expect of those closest to me? What do I expect of myself? And you? It is too simplistic to say that there are only a few expectations. I know I have many underlying hopes that I may not even be aware of at times.

Not all anticipation is equal. It is not all based on truth. It is important to know what my heart is hoping for in order to understand the source and the projection. In your Word, you have laid out your love in terms that are simple. When I live according to your way of mercy, I will find that the hope of your love accomplishing all it has set out to do will be fulfilled.

Lord, you are the joy of my heart, and I know that I will be full of gladness when you come through on your promises. Help me to know your ways and your wisdom as I walk this world with you. I align myself to your heart as I lean into you for strength today.

Strength to Go On

I can do everything through Christ,
who gives me strength.

PHILIPPIANS 4:13 NLT

God, in the trials and the changes of life, I am not left to fend for myself. I don't have to rely on my own abilities, power, and resources to get through. In fact, it is in my weakness that you become my strength. You have an endless supply of power that is always accessible through your mercy and love.

In your presence, I am saturated with your kindness and compassion. It refreshes me and brings me life. Where I am depleted, your Spirit floods me with unrelenting love that fuels me to do everything that I need to. You are the fire to my furnace, the gas in my tank, and every motivation I need. In you, I truly can do all things because you are the source of everything I require.

God, all my strength comes from you. My resources are quickly depleted, but in you I find what I need to go on. I lean into your love and you fill me with the power of your presence. What else could I require?

Fought For

The LORD your God is the one who goes with you to fight for you against your enemies to give you victory.

DEUTERONOMY 20:4 NIV

Some battles in my life are just too much for me to face on my own, Father. In every struggle, I have you fighting for me. You are the triumphant one who prevails every time. There is not a situation that is too difficult that you cannot turn it around. You can take even the most desolate circumstance and bring life out of it.

There are some things I am facing right now that feel like they are too much to handle. But I know this is not too complicated for you. You are my sustainer, defender, and deliverer. You go with me into every situation; you are with me now, and you will be with me when I need you. You will not withdraw and leave me on my own. I lean into your strength and find that there is more than enough grace to sustain me.

Defender, you are constantly with me. I am so grateful that I am not left to fight for myself. When I am overcome by harsh realities, you take care of me in your lovingkindness. Who can stand against your mercy?

Sustained by Love

Sustain me according to Your word, that I may live;
And do not let me be ashamed of my hope.

PSALM 119:116 NASB

When the storms of life toss me around, it can be difficult to find my grounding. Where are you in this, God? I may find it hard to see your goodness, but even in the chaos, you are full of peace. Your Word calms the wildest tempest and makes the sea like glass.

Your Word is full of light; it is sustenance for me when I am hungry. I will not be ashamed of my hope if my hope is in you and your faithfulness. When I wonder whether you are present, help me to look into history to see what it reveals about your character. When I look with eyes of faith, I will see you. Your goodness is inescapable, and your mercy cannot be exaggerated. What a wonderful love that sustains me!

Lord, you are the one who holds my life. You keep me even as I stumble. Lord, be the strength of my heart and the wisdom that I so desperately need. I depend on you to come through, and I believe that you will.

Healing on the Horizon

For you who fear my name,
the sun of righteousness shall rise
with healing in its wings.

MALACHI 4:2 ESV

As I live yielded to you, Jesus, I am covered by your wonderful love. When you walked the earth, you didn't just heal a few but all of the sick who came to you. You never turned them away. In the same way, you do not turn me away when I come to you.

I need healing, God. I trust that you who healed the sick and raised the dead will do the same for me today. You are more skilled than the most trusted doctor, and you know me inside out. I come to you with my pain today; you are the healer, and you will meet me.

Healer, touch me with your mercy today. Bring everything that is out of alignment with you and your kingdom back into alignment with your purposes and intentions in Jesus' name. You are incredibly kind and good, and I will not hold back from asking you. Restore me, Lord, and heal me today.

Thoughtful Living

Don't act thoughtlessly,
but understand what the Lord
wants you to do.

EPHESIANS 5:17 NLT

Wisdom is found in you, Lord. You are full of insight; your Word is an incredible guide to understanding your nature that is full of mercy and kindness. When I look for wisdom, your Word says that I will find it. It is compared to the most incredible treasure that can be found, worth more than rubies or gold.

When I seek to know you in relationship, I find that you are better than I could have ever imagined. Your love never lets go and your faithfulness knows no end. When I consider your attributes, I discover that to live like you means to consider others in greater measure than I consider my own desires.

Lord, I need more of your wisdom in my life. Help me to see from your perspective and to understand how it is you want me to live. I don't want to mindlessly live according to my whims. Empower me to live with purpose and mercy as my covering.

A Place Prepared

"Let not your heart be troubled; you believe in God, believe also in Me. In My Father's house are many mansions. I go to prepare a place for you. And if I go and prepare a place for you, I will come again and receive you to Myself; that where I am, there you may be also."

JOHN 14:1-3 NKJV

In a fast-paced world where life changes frequently and quickly, help me not to lose sight of the long-lasting values that remain unaltered, Jesus. You did not come to pacify the wealthy and stroke the egos of the powerful; you came to heal and save those who were needy and lost. Your love is boundless and knows no measure. It can't be bought or sold. You gives freely to all who would receive.

You have prepared a place for all of those you came to save. I am included in this. When I am struggling to believe, let my heart be open to your faithfulness. You have not failed yet, and you won't start now. I don't want to be troubled by the timeline; you are still working!

Lord, strengthen my heart to trust you. I don't want to be overwhelmed by worries. Flood my mind with your peace, my heart with your love, and my body with healing. Do what only you can do and make the wrong things right. Redeemer, show up and show off.

July

He will answer the prayers of the needy;
he will not reject their prayers.

PSALM 102:17 NCV

Champion Defender

He alone is my safe place;
his wrap-around presence always protects me.
For he is my champion defender;
there's no risk of failure with God.
So why would I let worry paralyze me,
even when troubles multiply around me?

PSALM 62:2 TPT

When troubles increase in my life, it can be difficult to not let worry overcome me, Father. You are described as a safe place; you are fully present with me, protecting me with the covering of your always-available love. You never fail. As I wait on you, I let my heart take courage in this truth!

Where I am overwhelmed by the distress of my circumstances, I turn my attention to your faithfulness. As David poured out his heart to you in the psalms, I pour out every emotion, every longing, every hope, and every disappointment as I experience it. I choose to look through the lens of your constant faithfulness in my life. Where I cannot see you, I trust that you will give me eyes to see where your deliverance is along the way.

Defender, you are the only one I can truly rely on. Where I fall short, where others fail me, you remain constant and faithful. I will not forget what you have done for me. Lord, stir up hope that I would trust you to continue to be present with me in every trouble I face.

Home in Him

A father of the fatherless and a judge for the widows,
is God in His holy habitation.
God makes a home for the lonely;
He leads out the prisoners into prosperity.

PSALM 68:5-6 NASB

Father, when I think of home, it should be a place of
rest and safety, of comfort and peace. Sometimes it
feels unstable and chaotic though. Thank you that your
household is a place of peace, tranquility, and ease. In your
house, I am completely welcome to be me—no pretending,
no self-protecting—just me.

You are a father to the fatherless; you set the lonely in
community. I am supposed to be united in your family. As
your child, I have space to grow and the freedom to grow
up in you. Where I have felt isolated and on the outside,
you have welcomed me in. I belong to you. I belong in you.
I belong.

God, you are my place of refuge and safety. You are my
home. Lead me into peace as I find my rest in your presence.
Teach me and guide me; love me to life again today.

Confident Help

We can say with confidence,
"The Lord is my helper, so I will have no fear.
What can mere people do to me?"

HEBREWS 13:6 NLT

God, life is full of unexpected turns. I cannot avoid change, nor can I predict what my life will look like in one year or ten. I cannot control whether others will accept or reject me. When it comes to my expectations, I can be sure that reality will often look vastly different.

So, what can I do? Should I throw up my hands in surrender? That is exactly how I can respond. God, you are unchanging in your love and wisdom, and you are never surprised by anything. I do not surrender to my circumstances and to fear; I surrender to your wisdom and leadership through it all. My confidence is in you, and you are always ready to help me when I need it.

Lord, my heart takes courage in your consistent love. You do not change from day to day. You are the same powerful, merciful God that you have always been and will always be. Redirect my gaze to your goodness when I am tempted to be overcome by shifting circumstances. I surrender to your ways, Lord, knowing your wisdom is better than the world's ways!

Restored by Rest

The LORD is my shepherd, I shall not want.
He makes me lie down in green pastures;
he leads me beside still waters; he restores my soul.

PSALM 23:1-3 NRSV

Left to my own whims and desires, I wander from thing to thing like a sheep left to meander on its own. I can easily lose my way and find that I have drifted from what was familiar and safe into the wild unknown. You, Lord, are a faithful shepherd who finds me and leads me to a place of rest for my soul. You always know the best way out of the chaos I find myself in.

You are a faithful protector, guarding me from the enemy that is waiting for an opportunity to destroy me. You are a place of refuge, and you keep a watchful eye on me. You give me everything I need. You are the perfect provider. Best of all, you never give up on me. You are constantly pursuing me in love.

Good Shepherd, I am so grateful to be yours. You lead me along the path you have prepared for me. As I follow you, you bring me to places of rest where you refresh me. I trust your leadership in my life. Thank you for never giving up on me.

He Is Near

The LORD is near to the brokenhearted
and saves the crushed in spirit.

PSALM 34:18 ESV

Father, it is not a failure to be heartbroken and
discouraged. Troubles in life are inevitable; they touch
everyone. I do not reflect your heart when I ignore
suffering whether that of others or my own. When pain is
overwhelming and I struggle to hope for anything better,
you are close.

Help me to sense your nearness in indescribable measure
today, Lord. You do not command me to be happy; you
draw close to the brokenhearted and save those whose
spirits are discouraged. Your comfort is mine here and now.
I am not alone. I want to feel how close you are even in this
present moment.

Lord, you are incredible in how you are drawn to the
humble and the broken. I will not hide my face from you
today. Come closer than my very breath. Fill me with the
comfort of your presence. You're all I have.

Guarded by Wisdom

Wisdom will come into your mind,
and knowledge will be pleasing to you.
Good sense will protect you;
understanding will guard you.
It will keep you from the wicked,
from those whose words are bad.

PROVERBS 2:10-12 NCV

Wisdom is not a vain pursuit, God. I may spend my time increasing my knowledge in various ways, but true wisdom is found in you. In your Word, I find keys to living in the light of wisdom. A good starting place is to look at the life of your Son, Jesus. He is wisdom embodied.

I need understanding, God, and human insight only goes so far. Help me to lean into you and ask for your perception over my circumstances. You have the answers and solutions for each problem that arises. I can trust you to guide me through every difficulty.

Wise One, guide me through the maze of my circumstances. I am at a loss and I need your wisdom. Breathe your revelation light into my mind and let me see from your perspective. Oh, how I need you!

A Thankful Heart

I have not stopped giving thanks for you,
remembering you in my prayers.

EPHESIANS 1:16 NIV

In the light of your presence, God, I find that what once went unnoticed is made clear. You have deposited your goodness in my life; you have not overlooked anyone in your mercy. When I ask you to give me eyes to see where you are working in my life, I can be sure that I will find you.

Gratefulness is a practice. As I stop comparing my life with others and begin to cultivate thankfulness for what is already good in my life, I will find my heart attuned to the frequency of gratitude. Small joys are not insignificant. They add up to a glorious inheritance if I keep count. Help me to appreciate both the seemingly trivial and the significant blessings that fill my life.

Good God, I want to see my life through your eyes. I have to believe that there is goodness to be found because you are present with me. Give me your perspective. Help me to look for your kindness in my life like I am searching for treasure. When I find it, I want to store it in my heart with the wrappings of gratitude.

Blessed to Trust

Blessed is the man who trusts in the Lord,
And whose hope is the Lord.

JEREMIAH 17:7 NKJV

Where there is confidence in my heart, there is a cord of trust. If I am confident in myself, then I trust that I am enough. If I display belief in others, then I expect that they are capable of what I imagine of them. When it comes to you, God, my confidence need never waver, for you are always shown to be faithful.

God, do my deepest hopes lie in my own abilities? Do they rely on others? I know for sure I will disappoint myself and others will disappoint me too if this is the case. I am not perfect but you are. You never wander outside of mercy and kindness. Your compassion does not shift or change. When my confidence lies in you, I will find that it is never dissatisfied. Help my heart to find hope in you, God. I don't want to give up or let go.

Lord, you are the keeper of my heart. All my days are before you. You are not surprised by anything. I trust in your unfailing love to hold me close and guide me. My heart is bound to yours in hope. I know you will not disappoint me.

A Father's Help

> The Spirit you received does not make you slaves, so that you live in fear again; rather, the Spirit you received brought about your adoption to sonship. And by him we cry, "Abba, Father." The Spirit himself testifies with our spirit that we are God's children.
>
> ROMANS 8:15-16 NIV

I rely on your help, heavenly Father. Thank you that I am not expected to provide for myself or fight those who would harm me. You are not just my help. You are my protector, defender, provider, comforter, wisdom-giver, and constant companion. Why would I try to get by on my own when you are ready to offer me direction and aid?

I do not need to venture out of the safety of your house only to fall prey to fear. I am part of a forever-family. I am not meant to get by on my own. I am not designed for isolation or self-preservation. Today I want to give up the fight of fierce independence. When I call out to you, Abba, you always answer.

Abba, teach me what it means to be your child. Thank you that I do not need to rely on my own strength or knowledge to be successful in life. I have found the belonging I have always craved and was meant for within your arms. Keep me close, Lord, and lead me as I lean on you.

Working for the Lord

Just as you have always obeyed, not as in my presence only, but now much more in my absence, work out your salvation with fear and trembling; for it is God who is at work in you, both to will and to work for His good pleasure.

PHILIPPIANS 2:12-13 NASB

In relationship with you, Father, I find how to live. Jesus displayed that ministry was always meant to be fueled by connection with the you. When I work, when I play, when I serve, and when I fellowship with others, I do it all as unto you. There is no obligation I have that is outside of love.

I don't want to be lazy in love though. Love is the fuel that gives me the strength to do all that is before me. I need not struggle to find within myself the passion to keep working. It is you who fills me and revitalizes me so that I do what pleases you! You are the pure source of energy that flows through me to reveal your love through my life.

Lord, partnership with you is an incredible mystery and wonder. You fill me with your love and mercy, and I get to give it away, constantly coming back to be filled again. The work I do is fueled by your grace. May I never go back to striving on my own.

God's Workmanship

We are God's handiwork,
created in Christ Jesus to do good works,
which God prepared in advance for us to do.

EPHESIANS 2:10 NIV

I was fashioned in your image, Creator God. It is in my design to reflect your beauty. There is no goodness displayed in my life that is disconnected from you. When I see the resemblance of love, grace, patience, kindness, and mercy in my life, I know that I am revealing you.

I am not a duplicate or cheap copy of a better model. You created me uniquely and wonderfully. I am not meant to be cookie-cutter. That was never the plan. But I was always meant for family. I belong to you. What I do, I do out of a reflection of you, Father. Help my life to align with the fullness of my heart which is overflowing with your compassion toward me.

Maker, you are so creative in your handiwork. You never duplicate your creation; not even two snowflakes or grains of sand are exactly the same. May I reflect your nature as I live out your incredible love. Fill me afresh today, Holy Spirit, with the fullness of your presence.

Rock of Refuge

My God is my rock. I can run to him for safety.
He is my shield and my saving strength,
my defender and my place of safety.
The Lord saves me from those who want to harm me.

2 Samuel 22:3 ncv

God, you are a safe place and shelter for me. You defend
me when I am weak and you liberate me when I am feeling
oppressed. When I have nowhere else to turn, I find that
you have always been the firm foundation beneath my feet.
I don't have to worry when I have you on my side.

When the storms of life rage and confusion covers my
head, help me to come to you for help. You are always
ready and you are never late. I want to trust you because
you have faithfully saved me every time. Your unchanging
character stands the test of time.

Defender, you are the rock of refuge I run to today. Where I
cannot see a way out of the trouble I am in, I trust that you
will guide me. You are my safe place, and I take rest in you.
Lord, come in power and rescue me.

God of Salvation

Don't hide yourself, Lord, when I come to find you.
You're the God of my salvation;
how can you reject your servant in anger?
You've been my only hope,
so don't forsake me now when I need you!

PSALM 27:9 TPT

God, you are near when I am brokenhearted, and you are close to me when I call you. You don't leave me to drown in my circumstances. You are the God of my salvation, and you will not forsake me. Even as I struggle in my desperation to find where you seem to be hiding, you will come through. You are already with me and you always have a plan.

When I find it hard to see where you are in the middle of my suffering, I will cry out to you. I know you will not be far away. You will surely rescue me, and I will sing of your faithfulness again. I take heart in this promise.

God of my salvation, you have been my only hope—the thing I've been clinging to. Don't give up on me now! Come close and bring relief to the chaos that has me swirling. I cling to you as I wait for you. Let me see you today, Lord.

Present Joy

Surely you have granted him unending blessings
and made him glad with the joy of your presence.

PSALM 21:6 NIV

No matter what circumstances I face, the joy of your
presence is always available. God, you bring life, joy, and
peace. And you also hold comfort and healing in your
hands. There is not a moment when you withdraw or
withhold your nearness. You do not pull away to punish
me; it is not in your nature to do so.

Today I want to find your nearness. You always have an
abundance of love to give. You are not a superficial giver;
you will supply everything I need and often you give so
much more! I draw near to you even now because I know
you are close.

My God, your presence brings life to my soul. I remember
the joy I found in you in the early days of knowing you.
Draw me to your heart again and revive my weary soul.
Everything I long for is found in you. You are my hope and
my home.

Slow Down

I wait for the LORD, my soul waits,
And in His word I do hope.

PSALM 130:5 NKJV

God, slowing down and waiting with a peaceful heart takes practice. It does not come easy in this day and age where instant gratification is the expectation. When I consider the important things in life, however, rarely do any of them come with quick returns. Relationships take time and investment as do fruitful careers and ministries.

Patience and perseverance are not popular topics for spiritual growth though I know they are necessary. It is in the stillness where I find the rest I am looking for, and it is where I often find what I would otherwise miss in the go-go-go of my busy life. With hope alive in my heart, help me to discover unexpected joy in the waiting.

Lord, as I practice waiting on you, I trust you to meet me with your goodness. Fill me with your peace and give me hope, teaching me to revel in moments of rest amidst the craziness of my normal life. You are worth waiting on. My soul finds restoration in you again and again!

Still Trusting

When I am afraid, I will trust you.
I praise God for his word.
I trust God, so I am not afraid.
What can human beings do to me?

PSALM 56:3-4 NCV

I cannot deny the reality of darkness in the world, God. There are wars and conflicts, atrocities and hatred being acted upon; there is brokenness and destruction to be found everywhere—from families to whole nations. And yet, you are light. You are truth. You are all-powerful. And you are present.

Where fear keeps me from seeing the bigger picture, help me to see from your perspective. You have not left me, and you are not worried. I dare to trust you today. You hold everything together, and you have not forgotten a single promise that you have made. You will fulfill each one. You will not let me be overtaken, and you will not let me be crushed. You are better.

Good God, you are the hope of my heart and the lifter of my head. Calm the anxieties of my heart as I trust in you. May your loyal love fill me up and cause every fear to be overtaken. You are faithful, Lord, and I find that your grip on my life is sure even when I can barely hold on.

Saved by Wisdom

Wisdom and money can get you almost anything,
but only wisdom can save your life.

ECCLESIASTES 7:12 NLT

God, your Word reminds me of the power of wisdom
especially throughout the Proverbs. Jesus' life is full of
the wisdom of the kingdom. When he taught about the
purpose of your law, he reduced it to its simplest form—
love. He instructed me to treat others in the same way
I want to be treated. That, he said, is the essence of the
teachings of Scripture.

This has not changed; it is still the standard. Does my life
align with this ageless wisdom? Father, there is no higher
law than the law of love. Help me to measure the success
of my life on this which is the foundation of everything
else. May love be the thread that runs through my actions
and my words. It is never too late to choose to walk in the
way of love.

Loving God, you are the standard of all that is good, pure,
and true. How could I but adore you when I consider
your incredible affection? You are not swayed out of
compassion or convinced to give up your relentless love.
May my heart stay bound to yours in this same love.

Divine Power

His divine power has granted to us everything pertaining
to life and godliness, through the true knowledge of Him
who called us by His own glory and excellence.

2 PETER 1:3-4 NASB

Your manifest presence, God, is found within the person
of the Holy Spirit who is my constant companion. I have
fellowship with you, here and now, through communion
with your Spirit. I have access to your power, alive within
me, giving me everything I need for life.

I need you today. I need strength, healing, and
encouragement. I need perseverance and patience. You
have everything I need and so much more. When I feel like
I am running low, you have more than enough to fill me to
overflowing. Come meet my needs—the small and the big
ones—with your powerful presence.

Holy One, I am so grateful that I am not left on my own to
suffer through life as a beggar. I freely come to you as I am;
you see me clearly. Fill me with everything I need today—
most of all the power of your presence. Restore me to life
again and breathe new hope in me.

Take Heart

"I have said these things to you, that in me you may have peace. In the world you will have tribulation. But take heart; I have overcome the world."

JOHN 16:33 ESV

Jesus, you graciously revealed what it means to live a life of surrender to the Father while overcoming the world. You showed me how to lay down my rights in the name of love—even in the face of suffering. I cannot escape the troubles and sorrows that arise from my human experience, but I can experience your grace and presence that leads me in peace.

God, give me courage to live with the same love that Jesus did. He conquered the world, and I get to rest in his victory. I cannot add to what he did, but I can live in agreement with it, refusing to strive for something that has already been accomplished. I have been brought from death to life and from darkness to light. I am no longer living in chains but in the freedom of your victory.

Victorious One, I rest in your triumph. There is nothing outside of your power. I align my heart with yours today, taking courage and strength from the same power that raised Christ from the dead. Holy Spirit, alive in me, I am your vessel. Fill me again!

Portion of Peace

"I am leaving you with a gift—peace of mind and heart.
And the peace I give is a gift the world cannot give.
So don't be troubled or afraid."

JOHN 14:27 NLT

God, you give gifts that others cannot even begin to dream of giving. The gifts are not contingent on what I have to offer in return. I do not earn them based on my achievements. Your kingdom is not a rewards-based training program. What you offer you give freely to all in the same measure—which is abundance! Your peace, which goes beyond my understanding, is a gift straight from your heart to mine.

I cannot earn your peace. I don't need to strive for it, and I don't need to wait for a better day to receive what is always free. Help me to receive your gift of peace in my mind and in my heart. Your peace calms my fears and anxieties.

God of peace, you are consistently better than I imagine you to be. What an incredible reality that you give freely without asking anything in return. I offer you my mind and heart today, and I receive your peace that reaches to the depths of my soul.

Seeds of Goodness

Let us not become weary in doing good,
for at the proper time we will reap a harvest
if we do not give up.

GALATIANS 6:9 NIV

In life, there are seasons of sowing and seasons of reaping. There are times of creating and times of tending. There are moments of great joy and others of great sorrow. God, no matter where I find myself, I know that you are the same faithful Father in every season.

When I continue in the way of love, as I've been called to, I will not always feel content in it. It is a narrow path, sometimes rocky, continually requiring me to lay down my own rights for the sake of love. When I keep going, living as one who has been marked by your incredible grace, I will be strengthened along the way. The coming fruit will be better than I can imagine.

Holy One, you see all my days clearly. When I am tempted to give up in my weariness, give me the strength to keep going. You are better than my best day, and more faithful than the rising sun. I give you today, which is all I have. Keep my gaze on you when my eyes begin to drift.

Never Without Hope

Those who love me, I will deliver;
I will protect those who know my name.
When they call to me, I will answer them;
I will be with them in trouble,
I will rescue them and honor them.

PSALM 91:14-15 NRSV

God, you are an ever-present help in times of trouble. You are the rescuer of the desperate, the defender of the weak, and a safe place for the wandering. You have never met a problem that you couldn't conquer, and there is no situation that is too much for you to handle.

Where I am struggling to have hope, please rush in and do what only you can do. You are my deliverer and my protector. You will rescue me. I may not be able to see how you will do it, but you will. You never fail.

Rescuer, I am so desperate for your help. Where I cannot fix my life, where I see no way out, I need you to come through for me. Fill me with your love and grace as I wait on you.

Good Gifts

Every good action and every perfect gift is from God.
These good gifts come down from the Creator of the
sun, moon, and stars, who does not change like their
shifting shadows.

JAMES 1:17 NCV

Creator of the universe—the Unchanging One—you are
the same one who is with me here and now in my present
reality. You do not vary in temperament or intention. You
are a good God who gives good gifts. When I consider the
goodness in my life, I can be sure that it is a reflection of
your love.

It is so easy to get caught up in the not-yets and the still-
to-comes. When I look at my life through the lens of lack,
I can easily become overwhelmed by discouragement.
When I start to recognize the things in my life through the
viewpoint of thanksgiving, my heart will be changed by
the encouragement I find. I want to take time to find the
good in the details of my life and be transformed by the
renewing of my mind.

Unchanging God, you are the giver of good gifts. Give me
eyes to see through your perfect perspective. When I look
at my life, help me to see where you are already at work. I
want my mind to be transformed by you. Fill me with your
love, Lord.

Extravagant Mercy

Celebrate with praises the God and Father of our Lord Jesus Christ, who has shown us his extravagant mercy. For his fountain of mercy has given us a new life—we are reborn to experience a living, energetic hope through the resurrection of Jesus Christ from the dead.

1 PETER 1:3 TPT

God, you have given me your own Spirit to empower me to live with hope beyond my understanding. My mind can only do so much. My heart needs to experience your love and the breadth of your mercy as much as my mind needs to understand. I am a whole being, and my whole being needs to know you.

Your hope is living—it has an energy! I want to experience your life within my body, spirit, and soul. Your life inside me is full of freedom. I can know this liberty that causes joy to erupt within me.

God of mercy, I want to know you with every part of me. Go beyond my mind and understanding; I want to know your love on a visceral level. Fill me up with your redemption life. I long to live in the freedom of your life within me.

United in Love

Be completely humble and gentle;
be patient, bearing with one another in love.

EPHESIANS 4:2 NIV

The fruit of my life partnered with yours looks like your nature toward others. Even though you were the Son of God, you were confidently humble when you were here on earth. You knew who you were, yet you did not make friendship with you difficult or exclusive. You often took time to honor those who were overlooked or despised by society.

I know that I am reflecting you when I choose love over everything else. In humility and kindness, not by force or arrogance, I reveal your heart to those around me. When I keep choosing to love those who are difficult to even like, I am walking in your way. Let love be the fuel of everything I do, God.

Humble King, you are the pinnacle of mercy and kindness. Today I align my heart with yours, choosing to humble myself and consider that I do not know everything. Lord, you see how much I need you. Fill me today that I may pour out your love to others.

Slow to Anger

Whoever is slow to anger has great understanding,
but he who has a hasty temper exalts folly.

PROVERBS 14:29 ESV

In the vastness of your love, there is patience, kindness,
understanding, and mercy. You are not easily angered or
set off. You are not on a short fuse. In your heart, there is
endless room for consideration and compassion. When
I exhibit slowness to anger, I reveal that my heart is
partnered with yours.

I have been shown incredible mercy by you, and not just
once but countless times! In the same way, I live out what I
experience. Help me choose to reflect the enormity of love
I find in you as I learn to connect compassionately with
others. I want to be someone who is full of peace, grace,
and understanding.

Father of kindness, you have shown your love in your
compassion toward me. I cannot deny the power of your
love that changes me. Fill me with your mercy that causes
me to slow down and consider others before hastily
reacting in my own interest. You are good, God, and I want
to reflect your goodness in my life.

Faith with Patience

Be like those who through faith and patience
will receive what God has promised.

HEBREWS 6:12 NCV

Father, patience in practice is never quitting. It does not mean perfectly believing and hoping in every moment. It does not mean never doubting. It is facing the challenge of the present moments that threaten hope and pressing through even if just by sheer determination. Sometimes it looks like being discouraged one night and deciding to keep going the next morning.

You are faithful to fulfill your promises. That will always remain true. Your timing, though, is often different than my expectations would dictate. In the face of waiting, help me not to give up hope. I will receive what I have been promised. I choose to keep believing even if it means wading through doubt on my way to the promise.

Faithful One, you do not change your mind based on shifting whims or desires. You remain constant in your intentions and loyal to your Word. I take hope in you as I press on. I believe that I will see your goodness in my life, Lord.

Alive in Christ

I have been crucified with Christ;
and it is no longer I who live, but Christ lives in me;
and the life which I now live in the flesh
I live by faith in the Son of God,
who loved me and gave Himself up for me.

GALATIANS 2:20 NASB

When I come to you, God, and give you access to all my
life, I find that you are the lifter of my burdens and the
freedom-fighter of my soul. You have set me free from the
chains of sin and death. I no longer live to serve myself
and my own interests; I've been grafted into your kingdom
where love's laws rule.

Where I see a lack of love in my life, I know that is an area
your presence can reach. It is an invitation for your love,
alive in me, to fill me with the power of your resurrection.
There is nothing in my life that is outside of the realm
of your great compassion. I invite you into my weakness
today and watch as you empower me to live.

Son of God, thank you for paving the way to the Father's
arms. You tore down every wall, and by your Spirit, you are
alive within me. I will align myself with your kingdom today.
Help my life reflect your goodness and character.

Tender Care

Warn those who are lazy.
Encourage those who are timid.
Take tender care of those who are weak.
Be patient with everyone.

1 THESSALONIANS 5:14 NLT

When I consider your fruit, it is all an expression of divine love, Father. Joy, peace, patience that doesn't quit, kindness that is lived out, faith that withstands the trials of life: these are all proof of a life that is submitted to your Spirit. When I look at the fruit of my life, do I find it is mostly self-focused, or does it point to your amazing love?

When I practice encouragement, caring for the weak, and patience with everyone who comes across my path, I am living in your way. The submitted lifestyle of a believer is one of overflow. I give away what I receive. Help me to come to you and receive the encouragement I need. I want to allow your Spirit to tend to me in my weakness. I want to keep coming to you and find that your patience never runs out. From this place, I can live out what I experience in living with you.

God, you are good. You show me how to live in how you act toward me. Fill me up with your love that I may live out of the overflow of the abundance of your heart!

Never Disgraced

Those who go to him for help are happy,
and they are never disgraced.

PSALM 34:5 NCV

God, you are my help in times of trouble. You are the foundation that I can stand on. You are the fulfilment of my longing heart. You are the same yesterday, today, and forever. You are always kind, forever merciful, and full of grace whenever I come to you.

I take heart in the truth that when I come to you for help, I will never be shamed or dishonored. Your heart is always full of compassion. You do not act in blind rage or annoyance. You are my good Father who always has words of wisdom to offer me. I need your help today and every day.

Holy Spirit, without fail, whenever I ask for your help, I have it. You know how weak I am; you are not surprised by my failures. I come to you and find an open heart every time. Give me the wisdom I need for the circumstances that are out of my depth. You are faithful!

Rest for the Weary

"Take my yoke upon you and learn from me,
for I am gentle and humble in heart,
and you will find rest for your souls."

MATTHEW 11:29 NIV

Jesus, you are so patient with me. You are the embodiment of divine love. I find belonging and rest for my weary, searching soul in you. When I come to you, you lift the weight of my heavy burdens, In your gentleness and humility, I find that though I don't measure up by the world's standards, I am fully known and loved.

I come to you today with my burdens. You are not waiting to berate my choices; you will not shrug your shoulders in response to my problems. Every solution I am looking for is found in your infinite wisdom. I want to learn from you and find the rest my soul desires.

Jesus, today I approach you with all that I have and all that I am. I trust that you will meet me with kindness and compassion. Lift my heavy burdens. May my heart find the rest I've been looking for in your presence today. Meet me and mark me with your love that changes me from the inside out.

August

I am praying to you because I know
you will answer, O God.
Bend down and listen as I pray.

PSALM 17:6 NLT

Words of Life

I will never forget your commandments,
for by them you give me life.

PSALM 119:93 NLT

God, your Word is full of instruction for my life. I can clearly see your character displayed through the ages. You are merciful and kind. You are full of love and compassion to all who turn to you. When I look for you, I will find you because you are always near.

As I turn my attention to you, I cannot help but find that your words are full of life. Where I feel like I am not measuring up, you lift my head and reveal that my worth is not at all dependent on my own goodness. You alone are perfect, and in you I am perfected. Where I have been striving, help me to find rest for my soul. I don't need to try harder to be loved more; I can never be more loved than I am in this very moment.

God of truth, in you is life, hope, and joy. As I meditate on your Word, I find that my heart is strengthened and encouraged to keep walking in you. What a beautiful revelation is your unending love. Fill me afresh with the kindness of your heart today.

Wonderful Destiny

This is no empty hope, for God himself is the one who has prepared us for this wonderful destiny. And to confirm this promise, he has given us the Holy Spirit, like an engagement ring, as a guarantee.

2 CORINTHIANS 5:5 TPT

Holy Spirit, you are my constant guide and companion. You freely give me the wisdom I need whenever I need it. I am not destined for destruction or destitution. Whatever I face in life, I do it with the strength and courage that comes from you. You are with me and you empower me with your abundant grace. When I begin to despair, you draw near and cover me in the comforting embrace of your presence.

You with me—this is my promise and my hope. Until the end of this life, I am never left or abandoned; I am not expected to do anything in my own strength. Help me to lean into your loyal love. You never change your mind about me. What awaits me beyond this life is even better than anything I could experience on this earth. This is my glorious hope!

Emmanuel, thank you for your constant presence in my life. When I start to fear for the future, remind me of your goodness and wonderful plans. May your presence be the strength I draw from in every circumstance. Every moment I am covered by your love. Fill me with your joy today.

The Victory Is His

The horse is made ready for the day of battle,
but the victory belongs to the Lord.

PROVERBS 21:31 ESV

There is no part of my life that is outside of your power, God. You are more than able at every turn and in every situation to do what I cannot. But I still need to prepare myself. It is a necessary and privileged part of life to work to an end. Most do not have the luxury of devoting their lives to passion projects while neglecting the nitty-gritty of necessary, mundane work.

There is honor in hard work, but I do not strive and toil for my worth. I do not work from a place of lack, but from the abundance of your heart. And when I have done all that I can, I am yielded to your ways that are higher. The victory is yours. It belongs to you. When I have exhausted my resources, I am fueled by your storehouse of abundance. I have access to draw from this place at any point. What a relief!

Victorious One, thank you for your power at work in my life. Give me eyes to see your goodness on display in my life in little and large ways! Today, I draw from your strength. You are the source of everything I need. I rely on you, Lord—don't let me down!

Abiding in Freedom

"If you abide in My word,
you are My disciples indeed.
And you shall know the truth,
and the truth shall make you free."

JOHN 8:31-32 NKJV

God, your Word is a light to my path. It gives me a glimpse into your heart, and it teaches me the way to live. Jesus, your life and ministry is full of keys to living a life submitted to the Father. When I follow your path of love, which is the harder way, I find life and freedom. It is so much better to follow you, where I am fueled by your compassion, than my own whims and desires which seek to gratify only myself.

Freedom is the ability to live unbound; I have the opportunity to choose what I do and where I go. I am unhindered by fear, lies, and self-imposed boundaries. The liberty that you lead me into is full of opportunity, growth, and joy. Help me to stay connected to your life through the continual surrendering of my heart to you. This is where I find everything my soul longs for!

Jesus, your life brings me so much hope for my own. I am yours, Lord. My heart belongs to you. I want to follow in your steps of love. Your ways are better than mine, and I know that living for you will not disappoint me. Fill me with the light of the revelation of your love.

Reliable Trust

Those who know the Lord trust him,
because he will not leave those who come to him.

PSALM 9:10 NCV

Lord of heaven and earth, you are constant and true. You are not reckless with your words, changing your mind from day to day. You are more reliable than the rising of the sun. Your heart of love is purer than the clearest waters. You are not a man that you should lie, nor do you withdraw your compassion from those who call on you. You do not change your mind about me; your affection is unfailing.

Sometimes it is easy to trust that your love for me is great. At other times it is a constant battle to believe. But I do believe that you are trustworthy and reliable. You will not leave me, and you will not fail me. Your mercy is abundant, and it is mine today.

Lord, you are unfailing in love. I submit my heart, my mind, and my soul to you today. I yield my own intentions to you because I believe that you are better. You're better than my best intent; your love gives me the strength to live out of love. You are good, God!

Healing Wisdom

Do not be wise in your own eyes;
fear the LORD and turn away from evil.
It will be healing to your body
and refreshment to your bones.

PROVERBS 3:7-8 NASB

My wisdom and knowledge is limited to my small understanding of a much greater, complex reality, God. When I submit my heart to you in humility, I welcome your perspective that is much clearer than my own. When I open my mind to possibilities that lie outside of my existence, I give myself the opportunity to grow in wisdom. When I listen and respect others, I also expose my heart to insight outside my own realm of reality.

God, you are full of insight, freely giving your perspective to all who ask. When I look for it, I will find it. Because your ways are higher than mine, and the way of love often costs me something even if just my pride, I find refreshing and healing as I follow your example.

Wise One, you never give stones when your children ask for bread. When I ask for your wisdom, help me to remember that the perspective I find in you is for my good. I submit my heart to yours, knowing that everything you do is fueled by mercy and kindness. You are not vengeful or tricky. You are reliable in love!

Forever Alive

The world and its desires pass away,
but whoever does the will of God lives forever.

1 JOHN 2:17 NIV

What an incredible hope I have in you, God. I do not live for this one, brief existence that passes too quickly. Though the world and its ways are momentary, my soul is not. I am an eternal being with the hope of an endless existence in your kingdom, my merciful God and King.

When troubles overtake me, help me to find my hope in you. Even if I face trial after trial and suffering after suffering, your purposes and heart for me are not negated. You are full of mercy, compassion, and kindness. You do not change your mind. I can be sure that though the earth decays and nations fall apart, you are forever kind, and I belong to you. Be the hope of my heart for as long as it beats.

God, you who are forever merciful, do not let my heart be overtaken by discouragement or despair. Give my heart the tenacity to hold onto your goodness no matter what is happening around me. You are better than my feeble mind gives you credit for. Don't stop moving, Lord. My hope is in you!

One Focus

I do not consider myself yet to have taken hold of it.
But one thing I do: Forgetting what is behind
and straining toward what is ahead.

PHILIPPIANS 3:13 NIV

Father, there is not much I can do about my past. Whether my upbringing was full of joy or trauma, my life has been shaped by my history and my choices. But that is not the end. What a relief that you are my redeemer. You are in the business of restoring broken things and making them new. As long as today is called today, there is still hope. You do not stop restoring me. You make all things new; it's what you do.

As I am made new in your love, help me to be encouraged to look at the goodness that lies ahead of me. It just keeps getting better. Even where there is suffering and pain, there is beauty to be found. I need not be discouraged by my past. When you come in, you fill me with everything I could ever dream of needing. I have not reached my end. There is so much more to come. You are my hope and the fulfillment of my every longing.

God, you are my one focus. I don't want to just get through my life; I want to live it with purpose, powered by your love that covers everything. Thank you for your covering of mercy. I can't help but be overcome with gratitude when I consider how you restore every broken thing.

Joy for Mourning

Those who sow in tears
shall reap with shouts of joy.

PSALM 126:5 ESV

There is no escaping the pain and grief that life eventually brings. Father, when loss rips my heart to shreds, it is hard to imagine that I will ever experience joy again. It doesn't help to pretend the pain away. Sorrow is as much a part of my experience on earth as pleasure.

I do myself a disservice when I expect to come to you only when I feel hopeful, confident, or happy. You are not surprised by my circumstances or at the agony that I experience. I discredit your love when I withhold my pain from you. You are the healer of the broken and strength for the weak. God, help me to come to you in my true state. You won't be disappointed in me, and as I let your love minister to me, I will find that I am not disappointed either.

Restorer, you give joy for mourning. A dark night is never the end; the sun always rises. You are with me in the intensity of my pain. You do not ignore the suffering of my heart. You minister to me right where I am and bring me comfort. Come close today, Lord, as I draw near to you.

Comforting Compassion

Let your steadfast love become my comfort
according to your promise to your servant.

PSALM 119:76 NRSV

The compassion of Christ is a beautiful picture of the comfort I find in your presence, Father. Your Son did not withhold mercy from those who were broken and wounded, but he healed them. He spent time with them, not requiring them to dress themselves up and come to the temple in order to find acceptance in his presence. Jesus, the humble king of heaven, met people where they were.

How could I not fall in love with you, beautiful God? Your requirement is the submission of my heart, lived out in love not perfection. What a wonderful mystery! Where religion requires the keeping of laws in order to be holy, you turned the system on its head. I find holiness in being united with you in loving compliance. Your holiness is mine, and I always find mercy and compassion when I need it.

Comforter, you are the one my soul finds rest in. When I fail, which is often, I find that you never change your mind about me. When my heart wavers, may your steadfast love strengthen me. You are the comfort I long for and the only one I need.

Until the End

> "Teach them to obey everything that I have taught you,
> and I will be with you always,
> even until the end of this age."
>
> MATTHEW 28:20 NCV

God, your ways are right and true. I follow you knowing that you will lead me into your goodness even when I don't understand the conditions of my circumstances. When I love like you do, I embody your character. I cannot go wrong if I live from that place.

As I follow your example, Jesus, I know that the path will not always be smooth. There will be times of pain. There will be hardships to endure. But I can be sure I am never alone. You are with me until the end of the age! There is not a moment or a day where you step away. Your presence is with me at every point. From you I receive everything I need.

Righteous God, you are perfect in leadership. You do not require what you did not give. A I follow you, Jesus, lead me in love. Strengthen me with the nearness of your presence even now.

Held Close

Even if my father and mother abandon me,
the LORD will hold me close.

PSALM 27:10 NLT

The strongest bonds I have on this earth pale in comparison to the strength of your mighty love, God. You are more compassionate than the most loving mother. You are kinder than the most merciful father. You are a better friend than the most amiable brother. These relationships are but glimpses to a greater reality—a stronger love than I can imagine!

Even if my mother and father disown me, you hold me close with your loyal love. Your affection never wanes even in the face of the depths of my humanity. You are infinitely better than I could ever give you credit for. When I feel isolated and I have no one to turn to, help me to take hope in your closeness. You pull me close and cover me in your powerful presence.

Faithful Father, you are better than anything I've known in my earthly relationships. Draw even closer and let me experience the goodness of your favor over me. I cling to you as you hold me.

Run to His Heart

It is impossible for God to lie for we know that his promise and his vow will never change! And now we have run into his heart to hide ourselves in his faithfulness. This is where we find his strength and comfort, for he empowers us to seize what has already been established ahead of time—an unshakeable hope.

HEBREWS 6:18 TPT

What an incredible hope I have in you, God. I run to your heart and find that I am surrounded by your faithfulness. You never back out of a promise. When the storms of life threaten my peace and the trials of harsh circumstances wear down my confidence, you are the place of comfort and strength I run to.

I am empowered by your grace to continue to trust and believe that all you say will come to pass. You have not given up and neither should I. You are bigger than my belief. When I falter in faith, you are still faithful. If I don't give up, my hope will not be disappointed. I want to be refreshed by your presence again today.

Loving God, you are the shelter from the storms of life. I depend on your presence to strengthen me in my weakness. Fill me with your love that pushes aside every fear. How they dim in the light of your goodness.

Light to See

The teaching of your word gives light,
so even the simple can understand.

PSALM 119:130 NLT

God, the truth of your Word is not found in complex theories. The gospel is so simple and yet more powerful than the most intelligent mind on earth. In the light of revelation, I see things more clearly. As I meditate on your Word, I find that the depth of your character speaks to every part of my life. There is nothing that is outside of your grasp. Nothing is hidden from you.

Your faithfulness covers everything. I can be confident in your promises; they are always fulfilled. When I start to doubt, help me look to your Word and even to my own history with you. I will surely see that you are a keeper of your word. You are with me at every turn. You are the light that brings clarity to every confusing situation. I want to continually look to you for my answers.

Yahweh, you are brighter than the sun. In you everything finds its rightful place. The chaos is returned to order in the light of your presence. Give me understanding where all I have is confusion. Light my path with your presence.

Not Disgraced

The Lord God helps me,
Therefore, I am not disgraced;
Therefore, I have set my face like flint,
And I know that I will not be ashamed.

ISAIAH 50:7 NASB

God, you are a constant help and friend. You lift me out of the places I get stuck in and keep me moving. With you as my defender and support, I won't be disgraced. You are more reliable than the most faithful friend I could ever have.

With you as my confidence, I can keep moving in the strength that you provide. I don't need to give up. But even if I do, you are with me constantly. You will not let me be ashamed as I work out my faith. Help my heart take courage as I rely on you to lead me through the maze of life. You see everything clearly; I can trust your perspective. I take heart today. You are my help and my companion.

Lord God, you are my shield and my portion. You are everything I need even when I don't know how to ask for it. Lead me on in your love and strengthen me as I walk with you. My confidence comes from your faithfulness. You are so good to me.

Generosity Returned

A generous person will prosper;
whoever refreshes others will be refreshed.

PROVERBS 11:25 NIV

God, when I look at your character, you are anything but
stingy. You are abundant in mercy, freely offering it to
any who would ask. You have more than enough kindness
to spare. You do not run out of compassion. You do not
make me jump through hoops to receive forgiveness. You
are always ready to pour out your love. You refresh me
constantly in your presence.

As your child, I reflect your nature when I give in the
same way. Am I sparing in my encouragement? Do I hold
back love from those I fear will reject me? Do I withhold
kindness from those I don't like? If any of these is true,
I want to change today. As I extend the grace I have so
willingly received, I am filled with even more. With you as
my source, I will never run out of love to give.

Merciful Father, you are so full of goodness that you give
away freely. Help me to live out of love, extending the same
mercy I have received from your heart to others. Your way
is so much better than my own. I align myself with you
today, being filled up to pour out and then be filled again!

Daily Portion

Fill us with your love every morning.
Then we will sing and rejoice all our lives.

PSALM 90:14 NCV

God, your portion is always measured out of your abundance. Your love cannot be contained in boxes with tight lids. I am your vessel, filled by you and also poured out for you. I will never run dry with you as my source. When I am lacking, I simply need to ask, and I will find that I am satisfied once more.

With your love filling me every morning, I have the strength and the sustenance I need to get through the day. I will go out rejoicing and return to be filled once more. Every moment is a new opportunity to be permeated by your compassion. I don't ever want to grow tired of it. How could I when it is life to me?

Loving God, you are so generous in mercy. I can't help but be thankful as you fill me up with your love again and again. Even when I grow weary of asking, you never hesitate to come through. You are abundant in kindness. Fill me this morning with a fresh revelation of your love.

Determined Steps

We can make our plans,
but the LORD determines our steps.

PROVERBS 16:9 NLT

God, you are over all and over each one. I can make my plans and follow through on my action steps, yet you are the one who ultimately guides me. When my plans fall apart and my strategies are flawed, your love leads me on. I don't have to worry about how I will get through with you as my guide.

Though I may be discouraged when my ideas don't go the way I expect, this does not affect your faithfulness. I see in part and know in part, but you see it all. You see the big picture as well as every detail. What feels catastrophic to me is not a concern for you. Help me find the peace I long for in the confidence of your goodness toward me.

Lord, you are faithful in all your ways. I bind my heart to yours, trusting in your goodness even when I don't understand. I bring you my questions, but most of all, I offer you space to do what only you can do. Breathe peace into my heart and mind; I open my heart to you again today. Speak, Lord.

Test of Time

All flesh is like grass and all its glory like the flower of grass. The grass withers, and the flower falls, but the word of the Lord remains forever.

1 PETER 1:24-25 ESV

In a world where everything has an expiration date, it is hard to imagine anything that lasts forever. You, God are eternal. You were before the beginning, and you will always be. When my hope is in you, it cannot be shaken for you are immovable.

In the light of what lasts and what does not, help me to be one who invests in the eternal. My flesh will die, just as the flowers fall and grass withers. But you will never fail. You do not decay. Your Word is forever true. Your faithfulness is without limit or end. Help me heart to find confidence in you, the everlasting one, who gives me new life. In you, I find undying hope.

Eternal One, your ways are right and true. I am so grateful that the suffering of this life is not forever. There is a much greater hope—life forever with you, unblemished and unmarred. My heart yearns for that reality even now. Lord, come with a taste of heaven's fullness. I open my heart to you today. Come and fill me with your unlimited love!

Faithful Protector

The Lord Yahweh is always faithful
to place you on a firm foundation
and guard you from the Evil One.

2 Thessalonians 3:3 TPT

There are so many unknowns in life, Father. There are twists and turns; I cannot control my fate. Even when things seem to be going according to my expectations, I cannot predict every situation or outcome. When I let go of the control that has always been an illusion, I give myself the freedom to lean into your everlasting grace.

You are faithful. You are the one who sets me in place. There are no mysteries to you. You are a reliable companion and a constant presence in my life. You protect and guard me from the enemy who seeks to steal, kill, and destroy. You come to bring life and not just a temporary fix. You are abundant in mercy, and you surround me with your comforting presence all the days of my life.

Faithful One, I lean on you. Guide me and protect me as I follow you. I let go of the need to control my own outcomes. I trust your leadership because I know that you are good. Fill me up with your grace today!

Seen and Known

God will never forget the needy;
the hope of the afflicted will never perish.

PSALM 9:18 NIV

There is not one part of my life that is unseen by you, Lord. Every need I have is clear to you. I don't have to worry whether you will come through for me; you always meet the needs of those who take refuge in you. Whether I see the way out of my situation or I'm at a complete loss, I put my hope in you. You are my ever-present help.

When I face problems that seem insurmountable, I know that you have every solution. You will not fail me and you will not let me fall beyond your grasp. Today I anchor my hope deep in your love that empowers me to trust beyond my own understanding. You are faithful to help me.

God, I take shelter in you today. You are where my help comes from. When I look around for answers, there are none to be found except in you. Be my rock of refuge. I hide myself in your goodness, knowing your presence will give me the life I long for.

Better Trust

The LORD is for me; he will help me.
I will look in triumph at those who hate me.
It is better to take refuge in the LORD
than to trust in people.

PSALM 118:7-8 NLT

When I look to people around me for security and affirmation, it will only go so far, Father. At some point, they will let me down. Even the most well-intentioned mothers, the purest-hearted friends, and the most loyal lovers will disappoint. The only perfect source is you. You are perfect in all your ways.

When you are for me, who can stand against me? You are a help in times of trouble—right here and now! When I take refuge in you, I am safe and secure. You will never let me down; it's not in your nature. When all seems lost and even those closest to me fail to meet my expectations, you are a better friend. You will faithfully follow through on every plan you have made. I put my hope in you.

Lord, you are trustworthy and kind. As I look to you, fill me with courage to hope in your name and in your promises. You always come through. May my heart's confidence be in your faithfulness alone. You are so good!

Freedom for Captives

"The Spirit of the Lord is upon me,
and he has anointed me to be hope for the poor,
freedom for the brokenhearted,
and new eyes for the blind,
and to preach to prisoners, 'You are set free!'
I have come to share the message of Jubilee,
for the time of God's great acceptance has begun."

LUKE 4:18-19 TPT

Jesus, you came to set the captives free. You led the way back to the open arms of the Father with your unmatched love that suffered the cross and the power that rose you up from the grave. There is no substitute for this kind of mercy. Where my heart is broken, there is freedom. Where I am blind, you give me new eyes. Where I am bound, you liberate me!

Your acceptance of me is unhindered and unmatched. Your Spirit is alive in me today. There is no chain that can keep me from you, and there is no situation too hopeless that you will not turn it around. Touch me with your power as I look to you today.

Lord, you are the miracle maker. You free every captive with your strong love. Touch my life with your incredible power and redeem all that seems lost that is meant to be found in you.

Unseen Hope

In hope we have been saved,
but hope that is seen is not hope;
for who hopes for what he already sees.

ROMANS 8:24 NASB

In the chaos of what is right in front of my eyes, it is hard to focus on what is unseen. God, you are near to the humble, and you bind up the brokenhearted in your life-giving presence. When I fumble in faith, still you are faithful. There is no challenge too great for you. You see clearly and in clarity speak from your unchanging goodness. You are full of love, full of hope, and full of joy.

When I lack in any of these, why would I try to stir them up in myself when I have access to the source of them? By leaning into your presence, I am filled with love, hope, and joy. Even when I don't understand how you could never tire of freely giving me your grace, I am benefitting from your generous heart. Help me cling to the unseen hope I have as I press into you and ask for more.

Great God, you are the source of all life. Nothing thrives apart from you. Be my hope, my joy, and my strength as I walk through this life. Fill me afresh with your presence today that I may draw directly from your heart.

Powerful to Save

Let us praise the Lord, the God of Israel,
because he has come to help his people
and has given them freedom.
He has given us a powerful Savior.

LUKE 1:68-69 NCV

Father God, you led the Israelites out of captivity in Egypt, and you are the same God who leads me into freedom today. Through Jesus I have been given access to you without condition. I am dressed in your mercy, and I cannot disappoint you because you see me through the lens of perfect love.

Where I am experiencing defeat, I know that you are strong enough to save me. You do not abandon me to fear and torment; you will surely lead me on in your kindness. You are a help to all who are in trouble. I call on you today; you will lift me out of the ashes of the old and make me new again in you. You make all things new including that which seems irreparable. I find my hope in you today; your power is at hand!

Powerful One, you are my Savior and my hope. When I tremble in fear and do not know where to turn or what to do, I cry out to you and you come to save me. It doesn't matter how many times I've needed your help; you are always quick in kindness and mercy. Thank you, Lord!

Taken Care Of

"People everywhere seem to worry about making a living, but your heavenly Father knows your every need and will take care of you."

LUKE 12:30 TPT

God of the stars and the seas, you can provide for my every need. You are the best Father; you take care of your children with the abundance of your resources. I don't need to worry about where my food will come from or about what I will wear. You will not let me go without sustenance or shelter. I don't want to hesitate to ask you for what I require.

Even in the midst of trials and suffering, you are nearer than I know. You do not abandon your children to the chaos of this world. Where I struggle to see your provision, help me to see where you are already at work. Where there is tremendous need, you are the God of miracles, and you will not let me down.

Good Shepherd, you are reliable in love and you always provide for every need I have. Draw near today in your presence, that I may know the comfort of your nearness and the warmth of your love. I need you more than anything, Lord. Encourage me in your presence.

Keep Going

I have fought the good fight,
I have finished the race,
I have kept the faith.

2 TIMOTHY 4:7 NCV

There is no defeat in this life that is final; though failures are inevitable, your mercy, God, is even more predictable. Perseverance is a virtue of following you, not because you are cruel but because this crazy world is. What does it take to keep going? When I have exhausted my own resources, I turn to you because you are abundant in everything I could ever need. In fact, what if I were to live from that place in the first place? Your life in mine is my strength and my joy!

Whether I am in a season of struggle or one of ease, I want to be filled with your strength as my fuel for living. When I don't know what else to do, I will lean into your heart that never changes. You are always abundantly compassionate and merciful, offering me the power I need to persist. You will get me through any and every scenario like you always have.

Holy Spirit, you are my help and my strength. I depend on your support in this life. When I struggle to even want to go on, come near and empower me with your presence. I am yours, Lord!

Mercy Cries Out

O LORD; give ear to my pleas for mercy!
In your faithfulness answer me,
in your righteousness!

PSALM 143:1 ESV

Lord, you are near to the humble and to the brokenhearted. Your mercy is never far away. It is closer than I know. When I fear tomorrow, the peace I could experience today is affected. Help me not to hold back from you. I want to take this opportunity to find that your nearness is the very courage and strength I need.

When I am overcome by the unexpected turns of life, it is hard to find my grounding. Help me to cry out to you; you never disengage! Your ear is always tuned to my voice, and nothing goes unnoticed. Whether with a shout or a whisper, you hear me. Even the unspoken cries of my heart are noted. I don't want to despair in the midst of the unknown. I choose to lean into you.

Merciful One, I won't stop calling out to you. You're my only hope! Where fear is threatening my peace, breathe your perfect love into my heart that stills the chaos. I am calmed in your presence. Come and be my portion today.

Tenderhearted

Be kind to each other, tenderhearted, forgiving one another, just as God through Christ has forgiven you.

EPHESIANS 4:32 NLT

Father, in this harsh world it takes practice to remain soft. Where my heart is prone to harden in defense, you have offered me a different way. When I represent your life, Jesus, it is not done with harsh speeches or cold distance. You were always approachable, ever near to the humble and the outcast. You didn't turn away from anyone who willingly sought you out.

What then should I do? How should I live? As one who is quickly offended? Help me to be as forgiving to others as you have been to me. Help me to stay tenderhearted in relationship, offering kindness and mercy where I am tempted to bruise with my words. As I have been shown incredible compassion, help me to freely give away sympathy with a heart that is in tune with you. And where I lack the desire to do this, help me to draw from your endless supply.

Loving God, you are better than any person I have ever known. Fill me with your heart of love that offers mercy freely. I want to look like you in love. I offer you myself again. May your love overflow from my life.

Radiant Truth

The precepts of the LORD are right,
giving joy to the heart.
The commands of the LORD are radiant,
giving light to the eyes.

PSALM 19:8 NIV

Your teachings are full of wisdom for life, God. They are not rigid rules to follow like soldiers falling in line in their regiment. Your principles are in perfect alignment with your wonderful nature. You are full of lovingkindness and mercy, and you give to all in the same measure. You are generous in compassion and never lacking in power to save.

When I consider your Word, I don't want to think about a list of regulations. I want to see an invitation to relationship. You are not a taskmaster who issues orders like a general. You have given us keys to abundant life in you through the life and ministry of your Son. Though I cannot avoid pain in this world, I certainly can benefit from the abundant grace found in partnering with you.

Gracious God, your ways are wise and your heart is true. You don't fluctuate in consistency. Why would I question your ways when you are constantly faithful and good? I align myself with you and your kingdom today. Empower me to follow after you and live like you.

Strong Joy

Don't be sad,
because the joy of the LORD
will make you strong.

NEHEMIAH 8:10 NCV

Father, there is not a moment of my pain that goes unnoticed by you. When I am overcome by sadness, I am not left to wallow in it. You come with the power of your presence when I look to you. You cover me in love, awakening my heart to the wonders of your goodness. When I have nothing to offer, there you are pouring out your compassion that strengthens me.

What a marvelous mystery—your joy fills me with the strength I need to keep going. And am I not your joy? You have abundant delight in me and in my restored relationship with you. I am continually filled with your powerful presence that never leaves me. The pleasure of your heart is the power of my life. What wonderful news!

Father, it is such a mystery to me that you are full of delight over me. I can't comprehend that kind of love, but I want to! Flood me with revelation to understand your affection in a new way today. There I will find my strength!

September

"Keep watch and pray,
so that you will not
give in to temptation.
For the spirit is willing,
but the body is weak!"

MATTHEW 26:41 NLT

Live Above Anxiety

"I repeat it: Don't let worry enter your life.
Live above the anxious cares
about your personal needs."

LUKE 12:29 TPT

God, life is found in yielding my heart to you. You hold me together. I do not need to strive to get everything on my to-do list done to be successful. When anxieties and worries flood my senses, help me to ground myself by laying down my life in submission to your love.

You are faithful to show up, faithful to provide. You will do what I cannot. I press into your heart of love today. I want that to be the fuel for my motivation. I will do what I can and leave the rest in your hands. You are trustworthy and dependable. Your love will never let me go or let me down.

Faithful One, I submit my worries and my cares to you again today. I know that you are more powerful than any doubt, question, or denial. Fill my heart with your hope that brings me life. As I trust you, lead me in your peace.

Citizens of Heaven

We are citizens of heaven,
where the Lord Jesus Christ lives.
And we are eagerly waiting for him
to return as our Savior.

PHILIPPIANS 3:20 NLT

Father, this world is not my ultimate home. I am not bound to a broken system and society forever. I am a subject of your kingdom, and your ways supersede the laws of this world. When I begin to despair at the brokenness I face in this realm of reality, may my heart be encouraged by the superior law of love in which heaven operates.

There is no height or depth that can separate me from your love. I am made fully alive in you even now in the waiting. Help my courage to be strengthened to live by your example, Jesus, knowing that your return is surely coming. You will not disappoint, and your timing is perfect.

Jesus, you are the hope of the nations and the expectation of every longing heart. I belong to your kingdom which is eternal. Fill my heart with your love today and teach me to walk in your ways of wisdom. May I be aligned in mercy and kindness, reflecting your compassion in my life.

Wonderful Plans

Lord, you are my God;
I will exalt you and praise your name,
for in perfect faithfulness
you have done wonderful things,
things planned long ago.

ISAIAH 25:1 NIV

God, your ways are higher than my ways and your thoughts are above mine. You are fully aware of every possibility and choice before me, and you are not worried for my future. You are full of wisdom for all who ask, and your plans faithfully work out time and again.

You are not stingy, and you do not withhold from anyone who seeks to understand your ways. How could I not praise you for your faithfulness when I look and see all that you have done? And you are not finished. You work in wonders and miraculously save your people. I am firmly planted in your perfect love that will not disappoint because I am yours.

Lord my God, I belong to you. Give me eyes to see your goodness where I have only seen my lack. Fill my heart with the revelation of your love at work within me, right here and now. You are better than my most vivid imaginings. Be glorified in my life and work out your wonderful plans!

Promise of Life

That faith and that knowledge come
from the hope for life forever,
which God promised to us
before time began.

TITUS 1:2 NCV

When I face trials and doubts, loss and great sorrow, it can
be difficult to see past the dark void of closed doors, God.
I cannot wish death or destruction away; in this life, I must
walk through the valley of pain where all of my doubts
creep out of the corners of my mind. But this is not my
downfall. This is not the end.

My hope lies in the promise of life forever without
confusion, pain, or destruction darkening my days. You
have promised me a beautiful eternity of fullness of life in
you. I come to you and you welcome me into your heart
and home forever without blame or harsh requirements. In
this short span on earth, I get glimpses of this glory, but my
present reality will pale in comparison to the magnificent
actuality of the kingdom to come!

Keeper of my days, you are the life inside of me. You give
me a glimpse of the glory awaiting me on the other side of
eternity. I am full of hope! Give me flawless faith to cling to
you, no matter what I may face in this short life. You are all
I have to hope in.

Confessed and Forgiven

If we confess our sins,
He is faithful and righteous
to forgive us our sins
and to cleanse us from all unrighteousness.

1 JOHN 1:9 NASB

God, you are merciful and kind; you are quick to forgive, like the patient and compassionate Father you are. When I confess my heart to you—even the pieces I try to keep hidden—you accept me and cover me in your mercy. I cannot be righteous on my own, but you cover me in your righteousness, marking me as your child.

Lord, I don't want to keep anything from you. There is no shame, no hidden flaw, no poor choice or series of them that can keep your love from pouring over me. It is always more than enough. There is nothing outside of your reach or your compassion. I bring you the wounded, tarnished parts of my heart and watch as you clean them up and restore them. You are more loving than I can imagine.

Father, I come to you with all that I am today. I don't want to hold anything back from you. Make me new in your love, covering every part of me and flushing fear out of my system. I invite you into my whole being. Wash me in your compassion and mercy. Refresh me in your living waters!

Born Again

All praise to God, the Father of our Lord Jesus Christ.
It is by his great mercy that we have been born again,
because God raised Jesus Christ from the dead.
Now we live with great expectation.

1 PETER 1:3 NLT

I have been born into your family, God, through resurrection power. The same power that raised Christ from the dead is the power accessible to me through your Holy Spirit. You are alive in me and with me in every circumstance. When I consider that mysterious and glorious reality, how could I bow to fear?

God, you could have called me a servant and made me do your bidding. And yet, you have always been about family and companionship. I am not a slave to fear; you are the King of love, abounding in compassionate mercy. My expectations are based on your goodness not on my experience. I will see your goodness alive in my life because I belong to you.

God, you are abundant in power that saves. Fill my mind with the awareness of your goodness at work in my life. I know that you are present; I know that you are with me. Give me eyes to see through the lens of your perspective that my heart may hope in you alone.

Led to Repentance

Or do you despise the riches of His goodness,
forbearance, and longsuffering, not knowing that the
goodness of God leads you to repentance?

ROMANS 2:4 NKJV

When I look at the world's leaders, Father, there is not much goodness and kindness to be found. Though I may find one, still all viewpoints are biased and actions limited. You, however, are full of lovingkindness toward all. You do not favor the rich or promote the powerful. You give the same portion to all—your abundance. You are close to the weak, strengthening them. You are near to the humble who have no other options.

How could I despise your goodness? Who am I to judge? I am led to your kind, welcoming heart with the same mercy you extend to everyone who approaches you. I am not punished by love; I am drawn in by it. Help me to be full of the same patient love and kindness as you are.

Kind God, you are the one who draws me to yourself in love. I find the freedom I didn't know I needed in your presence, where you make me come alive in your affection. I turn away from lesser things and offer you my whole heart again.

Detail Oriented

"Don't worry. For your Father cares deeply about even the smallest detail of your life."

MATTHEW 10:30-31 TPT

God, you are a master of details, not missing a single element. You are over everything. You are not too big to be concerned with the details of my life. You see it all, and not only that, your Word says that you care deeply. I so often get caught up in the particulars of my life while losing sight of the bigger picture. You do not have that problem.

You see both the big aspects and the small completely clearly. So, then, I need not worry. You are involved in the intricacies of my life all the while leading me into the plans and purposes of your heart for me. Help me to boldly walk arm-in-arm with you, trusting your leadership without apprehension. You are dependable and honest, always leading in love.

Holy One, you are wise in all your ways. I trust you with my life, knowing that you know better than I do. I harness my heart to yours; fill me with the confidence of your love and sprinkle my life with your goodness. My hope is in you, Faithful One.

Clothed in Dignity

Strength and dignity are her clothing,
and she laughs at the time to come.

PROVERBS 31:25 ESV

There is confidence that rises in me when I know who I am and what my life is aligned with. Belonging to the kingdom of heaven, I am clothed with strength and dignity. I have honor because you have given it to me, King of heaven. I can know that no matter what may come, my worth never changes. It cannot be altered by shifting circumstances.

Help me to be full of confident joy as I move throughout my days. Knowing that my value is not contingent upon my output or the condition of my life, I can walk with the poise of a dearly loved child. I am covered by goodness in every moment.

Wonderful God, you have covered me with your love and said that I am your own. What a glorious mystery! I am grateful to be found in your arms, my good Father, covered by your very nature. May I live with the confidence of heaven fueling my hope. You are so good.

Good Advice

Wise people can also listen and learn;
even they can find good advice in these words.

PROVERBS 1:5 NCV

In the wisdom your heart, God, lies every key to every question I could imagine asking. You are full of good advice and guidance for all who seek you. There is no mystery too great that cannot be solved by leaning into you. Though it is not an instant search for knowledge, the journey I take on wisdom's way will lead me along your path of goodness.

When I look in your Word for instruction, I will find it. Even more, when I get to really know your nature through your faithful Word and presence with me, I discover that the fruit often reveals the source. When I don't have explicit direction for where I should go or what I should do, I can be confident that you go with me, and I will know you are at work when I see the fruit of your love in my life.

God of wisdom, I hunger for your truth today. Fill me with your love that leads me to life. When I am not sure about the decisions I will make, give me confidence in your nature alive within me. Help me to trust that your Spirit will guide me, no matter what. I want to walk in your way, Lord.

Worship Him

Come, let us bow down in worship,
let us kneel before the Lord our Maker.

PSALM 95:6 NIV

Father, when I offer you the reverence and devotion you deserve, I align my heart with your good character. You are worthy of my adoration. You made the heavens and the earth, and you fashioned me with my unique traits that reflect aspects of your image.

God, I come to you with my whole heart open before you. I give you the honor that you are due. You are faithful and will always be. You are full of lovingkindness for all who see you. You are better than I ever give you credit for. I see only in part, but you are wholly divine and glorious. Help me set aside my list of cares and simply love you because you are worth being adored.

Holy One, you are worthy of all my praise and devotion. You deserve all of my trust; I won't hold it back from you today. Be glorified, Lord. Your love is better than life!

Led by Mercy

You in Your mercy have led forth the people whom You have redeemed; You have guided them in Your strength to Your holy habitation.

EXODUS 15:13 NKJV

God, you are the redeemer of the broken and rescuer of the weak. You are liberator of the captives and protector of the vulnerable. You lead me in kindness, never requiring more than I have to give. You are patient in love, always giving compassion to everyone who looks to you.

You are not weak in kindness. Rather, I find that there is incredible strength in mercy. You are powerful to save, and save you do! Help me not to be disappointed in your merciful heart that extends forgiveness to all. Instead, as I am lovingly led by your presence, may I find the power in kindness. Power to unite instead of tear down. Power to heal rather than injure. Help me walk in your footsteps.

Merciful God, thank you for leading in kindness. I want to be just like you! I will not hesitate to follow your path of love that leads to life. Teach me to walk in your way. I know that it is better than my own.

Followed by Goodness

Surely goodness and mercy shall follow me
all the days of my life,
and I shall dwell in the house of the Lord forever.

PSALM 23:6 ESV

God, your character is marked by your goodness. When
I look at my life and see through the lens of your mercy, I
find there is evidence of you all around. If I cannot see it, I
only need a shift in perspective. Your Word is a lamp to my
feet and a light to my path. Where I follow you, even when
I cannot clearly see, there is evidence of your life.

There is not a day where I am without your presence. You
are with me in the here and now, in every moment of my
life. I cannot escape your Spirit. When I turn my attention
to you in the present moment, I train my eyes to look for
you and my ears to listen for your voice. You have not
left me to my own devices. If I look, surely I will see your
goodness and mercy that are already here.

Present Lord, you are the one my soul longs for. When
I question whether I can go on, I am reminded that you
are with me. Where you are, there also is your love that
permeates everything. Open my eyes to see where your
goodness has been in my life. Your mercy is surely with me.

Keep Me Safe

Do not, O LORD, withhold your mercy from me;
let your steadfast love and your faithfulness
keep me safe forever.

PSALM 40:11 NRSV

I am kept secure within the safety of your unwavering love, Father God. Your faithfulness is my shield when I face uncertainties. You do not deny me kindness when I look to you. You are full of unfailing love that holds me up through the storms of life.

When I am desperate, it's hard not to let anxiety and worry overtake my mind. My nervous system responds to the stressors naturally. But you are my Maker. You know the intricacies of my mind and body. As I look to you, I will find the peace I long for. Help me fix my mind on your steadfast love that doesn't change with the seasons. You are the same yesterday, today, and forever.

Lord, you are one I cling to in the storms of life; I depend on you to carry me through when I cannot put one foot in front of the other. In my weakness, I rely on your strength. And when I feel strong, you are still the one who holds me. Thank you for your constant presence, faithful God.

Miracles of Mercy

Lift your hands and give thanks to God
for his marvelous kindness and for his
miracles of mercy for those he loves!

PSALM 107:8 TPT

When you show up in power in my life, God, my grateful heart can't help but praise you for your goodness. You do not fail in your love, and you never will. In the waiting, help me to remember your faithfulness marks everything you do. It is not foolish to hope in you, for you will always prove to be trustworthy.

When I see your provision and answers to prayer in the lives of those around me, I can celebrate with as much gratitude as if it were my own fulfillment. Watching you show up for others will encourage my heart on my own journey if I let it. Your faithfulness to one is your faithfulness to all. I take heart today; I will celebrate with those who celebrate and pray in believing with those who are still waiting.

Kind God, you don't stop working in miracles of mercy. You haven't changed the way you operate, and you certainly haven't given up. When I struggle to believe, may my heart be encouraged by what you are already doing for others as well as in my own life. Open my eyes to see your goodness where it currently is.

Carried by Love

In all their affliction He was afflicted,
And the angel of His presence saved them;
In His love and in His mercy He redeemed them,
And He lifted them and carried them all the days of old.

ISAIAH 63:9 NASB

God, you have never been distant. Even before Jesus arrived on the scene, you were full of tender care and love for your people. You have been faithful to me and you remain faithful to your Word. You do not leave me alone in my suffering and re-enter my life when I'm in a better place. You are constantly with me, carrying me when I cannot continue on my own.

What a relief that your manifest presence is always available to me. I am never left alone, and you do not expect me to drag myself through this life. I was always meant for connection, and I am always meant to eat from your table of plenty. I am not a beggar seeking crumbs and leftovers but your child that has unhindered access to a bountiful feast.

God, you have been my portion all my days. I have tasted of your goodness. Carry me in your merciful love when I do not have strength. I come to your table of abundance and eat my fill. You are so, so good!

Chosen by Compassion

"I will have mercy
on whom I have mercy,
and I will have compassion
on whom I have compassion."

ROMANS 9:15 NRSV

God, you are unendingly compassionate. Your mercy
has no beginning and no end. I cannot convince you to
withdraw your mercy from anyone—even me! You are
more loyal than the most devoted lover. Your tender care
is deeper than the affection of the most loving parent. You
really are that good.

Help me not to disqualify myself from being known as
yours. It does not matter how many times I fail; as long as
I humbly return to you, I am welcomed in. Once marked
by your love, I will always bear your signature. There is no
need to run from you when I mess up. I turn around and
run right into your arms instead.

Wonderful God, you are so much better than I give you
credit for. When I am tempted to withdraw from you, lure
me in again by your love. As I turn my heart toward you,
I remember your amazing love that covers all my shame.
Love me to life again!

Honored by Goodness

The LORD God is like a sun and shield;
the LORD gives us kindness and honor.
He does not hold back anything good
from those whose lives are innocent.

PSALM 84:11 NCV

When I was adopted as your child and brought into your family, God, I was once and for all covered by your mercy and cleansed from my unrighteousness. Hidden in you, my life is innocent. I don't need to worry about whether I qualify for your goodness. You are the one who qualifies me in the first place.

You bring me honor even in my deepest shame. When I let you minister to the dark places of my heart, your light shines and all that was hidden is made clear. You mend the wounds and bind up my brokenness. You are in the business of making things new, and you will do that for me. You don't just do it once; you continually heal, restore, and save. You don't grow weary of loving me to life.

Lord, you are abundant in love and plentiful in mercy. What an amazing mystery that you don't get tired of pouring out your love. My heart takes hope in that truth today. Here I am, Lord. Fill me again.

Peace to All

The Messiah has come to preach
this sweet message of peace to you,
the ones who were distant,
and to those who are near.

EPHESIANS 2:17 TPT

God your love is all-inclusive. There is no one left out of the kindness of your heart or the mercy that you extend. You came as a peace-bringer for all who would listen. And that is what you are. You give me the confident assurance of hope in the quiet knowing of my heart. Where there is chaos, I invite your peace in.

In the areas of my life where I feel out of control, I want your perfect love to fill my mind, heart, and body as I submit myself to you. Where I can do nothing, it is an opportunity for you to do something better than I can even imagine. Your peace is less like a quiet library and more like a sweet, joy-filled adventure with a loved one. It is unhindered communion, and it is mine.

Lord, your peace is so much better than the ups and downs of most of my relationships. You don't ever change, and you never argue your case with me. You are patient, kind, and true, and I want to be just like you. May I be a harbinger of peace in my sphere of influence.

Glory to God

Not unto us, O Lord, not unto us,
But to Your name give glory,
Because of Your mercy,
Because of Your truth.

PSALM 115:1 NKJV

God, your character is unflawed. There are no hidden faults in your nature or places of deception within your heart. You are faithful to your unending mercy and lovingkindness. When I consider your greatness, my problems feel smaller. In the light of your goodness, my flaws are no match for your relentless love.

When my heart is surrendered to you, your nature shows up in my life. I see your goodness, mercy, and truth, not because of how great I am but because of your greatness. You eclipse my feeble attempt to love with the expanse of your tender love. I don't rely on myself but on you. To you be all glory, for it is only through you that your mercy and truth meet me.

God, all glory be to your name. There truly is no one else like you. You are selfless in love, generous in kindness, and never lacking in mercy. What a wonderful reality!

Storms Stilled

He awoke and rebuked the wind and said to the sea,
"Peace! Be still!" And the wind ceased,
and there was a great calm.

MARK 4:39 ESV

When the storms of life rage, it can take everything within me to not panic and fear the worst, Jesus. When I consider that you calmed the seas and you live within me, I have no need to fear being overtaken by a storm. The same power that split the sea so that the Israelites could escape Egypt is the same power available to me.

You are not a one-time help in times of trouble. You are an ever-present help in trials and storms. You have always been with me and you always will be. My heart will take courage in your faithfulness; it will take rest in your power at work within me.

Jesus, you once spoke to the waters to be still, and the raging storm calmed. I need you to do the same in my life. Speak to the tempest in my soul to be at peace, and my heart will find rest. Where my life is out of control, bring order like only you can. I rely on you!

Fully Supplied

I know what it is to be in need, and I know what it is to
have plenty. I have learned the secret of being content
in any and every situation, whether well fed or hungry,
whether living in plenty or in want. I can do all this
through him who gives me strength.

PHILIPPIANS 4:12-13 NIV

Whatever circumstances I face today, God, I can be sure
that you will supply me with everything I need. You are my
provider and sustainer. Where I cannot see how I will cope
or get through, you offer me your unending grace that
empowers me to life.

I don't want to lose heart, Father. I will keep pressing on
and pressing into you. You never leave me on my own.
When I can't see a way out of the trouble you face, you
are with me right in the middle of it. Just as you were with
Shadrach, Meshach, and Abednego in that fiery furnace,
you will be with me. I take hope in you, my ever-present
King; you are the source of my strength.

Holy One, you are the hope of my heart. As my heart
trembles at the thought of all this life requires, I remember
that you are the strength that keeps me going. I cannot do
it on my own. Draw nearer still, Lord!

Truth Persists

The very essence of your words is truth;
all your just regulations will stand forever.

PSALM 119:160 NLT

God, your wisdom is pure and well intentioned. You are kind and merciful, and you do not seek to control me with blind rule following. Your teachings and principles are full of your compassion. You direct and guide me through your Word. You lead me in loyal love.

When I follow you and seek your truth, I won't be disappointed. Your thoughts are purer than my own, and your ways are full of wisdom. When I submit my life to you in humility and trust your intentions, I find that you always know better than I do. I may think my ways are good, but when I fail, I see that your discernment is a guide for my own good. Help me to trust in your truth as I follow you.

God, you are so much better than I am. My intentions are faulty, but yours are always pure and peace-loving. May my heart find strength to follow your lead even when it initially resists. Your ways are so much better!

Covenant Covering

I know that you will welcome me into your house,
for I am covered by your covenant of mercy and love.
So I come to your sanctuary with deepest awe
to bow in worship and adore you.

PSALM 5:7 TPT

It is a wonderful gift that you have welcomed me into your house, Creator of life. I don't come by my own merit; I don't earn entrance by my good deeds. It is your covenant of mercy that covers me. You have done everything necessary to welcome me into your presence, and I need only come to you.

I can't help but be transformed by your goodness that covers me. Your incredible love wraps around me like a blanket, comforting me and bringing me rest. What a wonder that the belonging I am looking for has nothing to do with what I offer. I simply enter into this relationship and reap all of the benefits. As I am changed, I reflect this same kind of mercy and goodness to others.

Lord, thank you for your covering that allows me to enter your presence. I can't help but adore you when you are indescribably good. Fill me with your mercy that I may embody it in my life. I'm so thankful for your incredible love that changes everything.

Cling to God

You shall fear the LORD your God;
you shall serve Him and cling to Him,
and you shall swear by His name.

DEUTERONOMY 10:20 NASB

When I walk in your way, Lord, which is the path of love,
your goodness and mercy are all over my life. I cannot
follow you and be left out of the covering of your love.
It's just not possible. Sometimes it is hard for me to see
what is around me in the dark. As I cling to you, allowing
you to lead me through the black of night, I cannot clearly
understand what, if anything, is growing. When the day
breaks and the sun rises, I will see that your goodness has
been there all along even when I could not comprehend it.

Help me not to lose hope when I am experiencing a dark
night. On the other side, I will see evidence of your mercy
every step of the way. You are trustworthy. I hold on to you
and keep moving forward.

Father, I rely on you to come through for me again and
again. I cannot escape your goodness even if I try! When
your light shines on my life, I see the treasures that were
hidden in darkness all along. You are my strength, Lord. I
depend on you.

Turn to Me

Answer me, O LORD, for your steadfast love is good;
according to your abundant mercy, turn to me.

PSALM 69:16 NRSV

There is no end to your mercy, Father. Your steadfast
love has no interruption, and there is nothing I can do to
talk you out of your compassion. When my heart needs
to remember your goodness, should I not recount your
faithfulness? You have been constant through the ages,
consistent in kindness.

I need a touch from you today, Lord. My heart needs you. I
want to remember your goodness to others and to me so I
can stir up hope again. You are more than able, more than
willing, to meet me right where I am today. I don't have to
clean myself up or dress up my unbelief. According to your
unfailing love and overflowing mercy, you will meet me.

Holy One, you are the one I come to in the hour of my need
and in the time of my rejoicing. You see my heart, just as it
is right now in this moment. Meet me with your love, Lord.
I can't pretend that I don't desperately need it. Here I am;
meet with me.

Blessed to Receive

"Blessed are the merciful,
for they shall receive mercy."

MATTHEW 5:7 NASB

One of the principles of your kingdom, God, is that with the same measure I use, it will be shown to me. If I refuse to show mercy to others, mercy will be withheld from me. If I do not forgive others, how can I receive forgiveness? If I don't make room for more by giving away what I have, then there is no space to receive. You are bigger, even than these principles, but why would I want to withhold something that has been so freely given to me?

In love, I choose to love others. I want my heart to be filled up as I pour out. God, you don't leave me dry, and you don't expect me to budget my love. Your heart is always full to overflowing. Why would I operate as one who has a limited supply when my source is the Source of all life? I want to live generously, for in generosity I will receive.

Merciful God, you are full of lovingkindness. Even as you pour out more, you never diminish in compassion. You are my supply! Fill me up that I may pour out, and I will return for more. You are so generous, Lord.

Kind God

The LORD is righteous in everything he does;
he is filled with kindness.

PSALM 145:17 NLT

In all things, God, you are good. You are better than the most reliable, kind-hearted, forgiving person I could ever know. You never shift in consistent love. The more I get to know you in relationship, the more I find that you are better than I could have ever imagined.

I can trust your ways because I know your amazing nature. The things that hold me back from you are limited; they don't complete the whole picture. When I surrender my understanding and see from your perspective, I align with you in trust. Your love is pure and I can depend on it all the days of my life.

God, you are kind in all of your ways. Your patience reflects this—even just your patience with me! I believe that you are better than I have even tasted. I surrender to your ways, Lord. Fill my life with your wisdom, peace, and truth.

Image of Love

"Love your enemies, do good to them, and lend to them without expecting to get anything back. Then your reward will be great, and you will be children of the Most High, because he is kind to the ungrateful and wicked."

LUKE 6:35 NIV

Your mercy, God, is always freely given with no conditions. When I live with the same kind of generosity, I find that I am reflecting you. Your path of love is not the easier way to live because it constantly calls my ego into submission. When I lay down my rights, I will find the life that the Spirit imparts to me is so much better than the pride I could find in my own success.

When I consider a life of kindness, without expecting an immediate return for my investment, it seems strange. There is a reward awaiting those who live humbly, loving others without agenda, and it is straight from your hand. I want my heart to consider what love's image looks like in my life.

Most High, you are the way, the truth, and the life. Your ways are so much better than my own; I won't run away from your love, and I won't hold back from your heart. Strengthen and empower me to follow after you no matter what.

Heard

The LORD does not listen to the wicked,
but he hears the prayers of those who do right.

PROVERBS 15:29 NCV

To be right with you, God, I simply need to submit my heart to you and ask you to cover me in your love. You will wash away every blemish and stain that keeps me from seeing your goodness. The wicked are full of pride and think they know everything, but the humble admit that there are things outside of the realm of their understanding. I want to be humble.

I approach your throne of grace with boldness, knowing that you hear me. And if you hear me, surely you will answer me. You are faithful in love and mercy, always extending kindness. I don't need to fear that you will ignore me, or worse, turn me away. It is not in your nature to deny compassion to a seeking heart. You are always reaching out in love—always!

Lord, I have no goodness on my own, but in you I see redemption and life all around me. I depend on you to transform the broken, chaotic parts of my life. I know that restoration is yours alone. God, come and make all things new in my life.

October

Answer me when I pray to you,
my God who does what is right.
Make things easier for me
when I am in trouble.
Have mercy on me
and hear my prayer.

PSALM 4:1 NCV

Living Expression

The Living Expression became a man and lived among us! And we gazed upon the splendor of his glory, the glory of the One and Only who came from the Father overflowing with tender mercy and truth!

JOHN 1:14 TPT

Jesus, you are the full expression of God. You were God from the beginning, and you confined yourself to flesh and bones so I could know the fullness of your love lived out in human form. When I lack wisdom, I can look to your example. You weren't just a model for relationship with the Father, you are the fulfillment of every hope I have. You were, you are, and you always will be.

Your story didn't end at the cross or the grave. In your resurrection, you were raised to life forever, and you once and for all defeated the curse of death over me. I am raised to life in you, first by fellowship with you, and second when this life is over and you redeem everything. What a hope and foundation this is for me. Help my heart to find encouragement in your legacy here and now.

Merciful God, you are full of tenderness toward me. Your truth supersedes my logic and understanding. Fill me with the revelation of your wisdom. I want to walk in your ways, truly knowing your heart. Help me where I fail to understand and give me tenacity to trust in every circumstance.

Peace with God

Since we have been justified by faith,
we have peace with God
through our Lord Jesus Christ.

ROMANS 5:1 ESV

When I have a bad day, God, it affects how I view my relationships. Sometimes I find myself uncomfortable with myself and others. Thank you that you never change your mind about me. Because I have submitted my life to you, I can have peace with you, and not even the worst day full of my poorest choices can change that.

Thank you that I do not rely on my perfection to find peace in you. You freely give me mercy, and I can never deplete your resources. Where troubles have me on edge, help me to look to the reality of your goodness to calm my anxieties. I am yours and you love me.

Good God, thank you for being the one who does all the heavy lifting in this relationship. I am perfected in you, covered by unfailing love. Refresh me again in your presence where my heart is brought alive in you. I need you more than the air I breathe.

Kingdom of God

The kingdom of God is not eating and drinking,
but righteousness and peace and joy
in the Holy Spirit.

ROMANS 14:17 NASB

When I am overly concerned by my needs, it can be difficult to feel at peace. Thank you, God, that you have an endless supply within your kingdom available to me through your presence. Your Holy Spirit is the conduit of never-ending grace, peace, and joy.

God, when I am lacking, all I have to do is ask you. You will not leave me dry when I call on you for hope, joy, peace, or anything else I need. You are so much more than a provider though you certainly never leave me wanting. Your Spirit is always with me, freely filling me with your goodness. I invite you to meet with me today with the abundance of your love. As you draw near, I will not be disappointed.

God, your kingdom is so much better than the courts of the most lavish kingdoms on earth. Though rulers feast on the finest foods, I have access to something even better—the fullness of joy, peace, and love through your Spirit at every moment! Fill me again today, Lord.

Watched Over

The LORD keeps you from all harm
and watches over your life.
The LORD keeps watch over you as you come and go,
both now and forever.

PSALM 121:7-8 NLT

Fear is a strong force that either keeps me stuck, propels me into hasty decisions, or causes me to run away. Perfect love is full of clarity, wisdom, and the freedom of choice. It is unhurried and peaceful. There is power in the stillness it provides to the chaos. Lord, you are rich in love, not wishing for anyone to waste away in torment. Where fear has been a motivator, I ask your rich mercy to overtake it.

You see my every step. You do not turn away as I move through life; you don't miss a moment. You are the keeper of all of my days. I don't want fear to be the driving force of my life. I want your love and wisdom to be my guide. I know the difference by the fruit of my heart and life. Where there is peace, you are there. I press into your peace today.

Lord, you are the keeper of my life. I know that you see me and you walk with me. You keep me from harm as I walk in the way of love, choosing your wisdom over my own. Where fear has overtaken aspects of my life, I ask for your perfect love and peace to replace it. I receive your kindness over every area.

Looking Up

To you I lift up my eyes,
O you who are enthroned in the heavens!

PSALM 123:1 NRSV

Father, my pace of life is incredibly hurried. There is always more to do, and since I am often connected digitally, there is pressure to perform in unreasonable ways at an extreme pace. There are countless demands on my attention even recreationally. I need never take the time to pause and reflect, or to set down my phone in order to observe the world around me. But this is not how I was meant to function. I need fresh air and other people. I need time and space to rest without the nagging of potential projects in the back of my mind.

Help me to take more than a few minutes to step away from the demands of life and just rest. Draw my gaze up to the heavens. Whether cloud-watching by day or gazing at the stars, when I direct my gaze upwards, it brings a shift in my perspective.

God, you are enthroned in the heavens, yet even they can't contain you! You are so much bigger than my little life, but you are still concerned with me. My heart is relieved when I think about how much greater than me you are; I find hope in your power and higher perspective.

Satisfied in Him

They shall neither hunger nor thirst,
Neither heat nor sun shall strike them;
For He who has mercy on them will lead them,
Even by the springs of water He will guide them.

ISAIAH 49:10 NKJV

God, you are perfect in mercy and abundant in power to save. You guide me with your wise leadership. You provide for every need. I will not go hungry or thirsty. You protect me from the harsh elements, and you lead me on paths of peace in your presence.

Your way is the way of love. Sometimes it seems too good to be true. I cannot bypass pain in this life; yet, even as I walk through it, you are my provider. You are my shelter. Your mercy never fails; it is always more than enough for everything I face. I walk in communion with you, the Creator, as my guide. What a wonderful gift!

Merciful God, my soul finds everything it needs in you. I am satisfied by your persistent presence that fills me with goodness beyond my imaginings. Lead me in your perfect wisdom, Lord. I am yours!

Answer Me

O LORD; give ear to my pleas for mercy!
In your faithfulness answer me, in your righteousness!

PSALM 143:1 ESV

When I grow weary in my circumstances, reliving the same cycles over and over, it can be difficult to keep asking you for healing and redemption, Father God. When I find it hard to hope, help me not to abandon faith. I want to keep pressing into you even when I can't see the way out.

You are always faithful. You don't change your character based on the length of my troubles or the attitudes I have concerning them. You are so much better than that. Your love is constant in every circumstance. Where I struggle to see the light of your goodness in my life, help me to never stop crying out for your help. You are always nearer than I know.

Lord, you are my saving grace and the help I rely on. There is no one like you. Do you see my desperation? I can't hold back my cries for your mercy to show up again in my life. I depend on your faithfulness like I need water to survive!

Renewed

He saved us, not on the basis of deeds
which we have done in righteousness,
but according to His mercy,
by the washing of regeneration
and renewing by the Holy Spirit.

TITUS 3:5 NASB

God, your ways are without equal in this world. You are full of compassion for all, never turning away a hungry heart. You will not let the helpless be overrun by evil. Salvation is through you alone. I don't need to dress myself up or be a high achiever to earn your mercy. It is a free gift, provided straight from your presence.

Your Holy Spirit cleanses and renews me with your kindness. It's not anything I've done—it's all you. What an amazing reality that you cover me in pure love. I am filled with the power of your presence that awakens my heart to life. You minister to my wounds, reaching the depths of me. You heal my broken heart. Continue to change me from the inside out with your wonder-working Spirit.

Holy Spirit, you breathe life into me and awaken parts of my soul that I thought were gone forever. You restore the innocence of my inner child and give me eyes to see my past through your faithfulness. You are so good. Don't ever stop doing your wonderful work in my life.

Springs of Life

How priceless is your unfailing love, O God!
People take refuge in the shadow of your wings.
They feast on the abundance of your house;
you give them drink from your river of delights.
For with you is the fountain of life;
in your light we see light.

PSALM 36:7-9 NIV

God, you are a refuge for the weak, abundant provision for the needy, and full of delight for those who drink from your presence. When I look to you, I find that things in life become clearer. Questions are answered and solutions reveal themselves. In your love, I will never find myself lacking any good thing.

When I feel overrun by the troubles of life, I run into your love. Your presence will never fail to both guard and strengthen me. I drink from your river of delights. When I can only bring you my sadness, help me not to be discouraged. You will wrap your presence around me with the comfort I need and fill my soul with the sweetness of your heart.

Unfailing One, you are the one I cling to. I come to you with all my lack, every need, and the raw reality of my emotions today. I know they are not too much for you. Surround me in your presence and satisfy my heart with the kindness of yours.

Dazed with Despair

My inner being is in depression
and my heart is heavy, dazed with despair.

PSALM 143:4 TPT

Depression is not a new phenomenon. The worries of this world have always been heavy. The burden of suffering is an age-old experience. When sadness follows me like a gray cloud, God, it sometimes feels as if the sun will never shine again. But my feelings do not predict your faithfulness. What good news that is! The light will shine on me again; it will burn away the fog of despair.

When my heart is heavy, help me to find comfort in your arms. Your Spirit is my comforter, and he is nearer than the breath in my lungs. You will not let me go—not ever! You are the lifter of my burdens, and you share your strength with me whenever I need it. Even today you are close.

Holy One, surround me with the comfort of your presence, and come nearer than you've ever been. May I taste the goodness of your heart today—I know that it is sweet. Override the worries that swirl around my mind with your perfect peace. You are the lifter of my burdens

Victory

Every child of God defeats this evil world,
and we achieve this victory through our faith.

1 JOHN 5:4 NLT

My life is hidden in you, Jesus. Every failure and every success is covered by you. I need not despair my disappointments when you are where my ultimate triumph is found. You have equipped me with everything I need to live an abundant kingdom life. You always give in generosity and not begrudgingly.

I am your child, God, and as such, I belong to your family and I inherit the fruit of your kingdom. I will not be overcome with evil, but I will overcome evil with good. That is your promise to me. I find my strength in you today. You will not leave me without.

God, as your child, I rely on your power to strengthen me to live with your goodness pouring out of my life. Even when I cannot see it, I know that you are working within me because I am yours! You are my victory, and you never, ever fail.

Kindness Matters

Kind people do themselves a favor,
but cruel people bring trouble on themselves.

PROVERBS 11:17 NCV

In a power-driven world, kindness is often brushed off as weakness. The ways of this world are marked by ease and efficiency, while the ways of your kingdom are marked by mercy and peace, God. The world is about tasks and your kingdom is about relationships. This is not to say that nothing gets done when I follow you, but the importance is always on relationship. People always come before work.

I know I should love you and others as I love myself. When worth is an inherent value in humanity rather than a reflection of what a person has to offer, kindness is a natural reaction. Help me to be full of compassion in my interactions with others.

Compassionate One, you are full of kindness to all. As your child, I want to reflect that same mercy in my own life. Where I am prone to overlook others in favor of my own agenda, gently remind me of the most worthwhile endeavor—to love.

Grace Given

"I will make all my goodness pass before you and will proclaim before you my name 'The Lord.' And I will be gracious to whom I will be gracious, and will show mercy on whom I will show mercy."

EXODUS 33:19 ESV

When I look for you, God, I find you. You do not stay hidden when I am searching for your goodness. You are endlessly compassionate. You cannot be talked out of your mercy. You are incredibly kind in your dealings with me, and you often give me much more than I ask for.

I want to trust your wisdom in my life. You do not require my obedience for your own sake. You don't need me to fall in line and blindly follow your regulations. What you want—what you have always wanted—is companionship. What a wonder that I can know you in the beauty of your goodness. Your wisdom is for my good, and that is always the case. Help me to trust your ways because I trust your heart.

Gracious God, you are beautiful in your mercy. Thank you for freedom to know you. As I draw near, you come closer still. Lead me in the power of your present love today.

Faithful God

Know that the LORD your God, He is God, the faithful
God who keeps covenant and mercy for a thousand
generations with those who love Him
and keep His commandments.

DEUTERONOMY 7:9 NKJV

God, often I realize that I have completely forgotten about
a memory until someone else mentions it. I probably
don't spend enough time remembering things in my life.
There are so many things that slip my consciousness. As
I practice recollection, I know I will be surprised at the
beauty I rediscover.

Your faithfulness is a marker of your character; it never
changes, and you never fail to keep your covenant. As I
look through my history with the lens of your loyalty, my
heart will inevitably fill with gratitude. You who have done
it before will do it again. You won't ever stop.

Faithful One, give me eyes to see where you have been
working in the story of my life up until now. I want to see
from your perspective. Spirit, open my heart to yours as I
look for you. I know that you hear me. You are so faithful.

Abundant Peace

May mercy, peace, and love
be yours in abundance.

JUDE 1:2 NRSV

In a world where I fight scarcity on multiple levels—
emotionally, physically, and mentally—a God who freely
gives in quantities of abundance feels like a foreign
concept, Father. You don't just give me enough to survive
in the moment, you give more than I need in most cases!

Where I am longing for peace, you grant it freely. Where I
need mercy to meet me, there it is in plenty. Where my dry
soul longs for love, there is a river of compassion flowing
toward me. As I receive from your generous heart, I can't
help but begin to act with the same approach to others. I
won't become a whole version of myself by accident; I am
filled to overflowing with the goodness of your Holy Spirit
who transforms me.

Good God, you are my portion of mercy, love, and peace.
The measures you use are not the same as the world's, and
for that I am beyond thankful! There is always more than
enough to both receive and to give away. Your love is full; it
is rich and satisfying.

Wholeness in Him

May the God who gives us his peace and wholeness
be with you all. Yes, Lord, so let it be!

ROMANS 15:33 TPT

God, in a world of competition and never enough, I find
that I am sometimes dissatisfied with what is good in
my life; I'm always looking to what could be better. The
problem with this is that I miss what is already wonderful.
How will I ever be satisfied later if nothing is good enough
in the here and now?

Father, you are present in this very moment. Your peace
can be mine right now. If the fullness of your presence is
mine, then I have everything that is good available to me
right here. You are wholly accessible in this moment, and in
your I am made whole. Why do I wait to obtain something
later when it is mine for the taking now? Help me to press
into you today and find every longing satisfied in your
presence.

God, you are the one who brings healing and wholeness. I
don't want to waste another moment waiting for the right
time, when the right time is now. You are good, you are
here, and you are mine. Come and fill me, Lord. Not with a
portion, but with the fullness of your presence.

Dependent on God

It depends not on human will or exertion,
but on God, who has mercy.

ROMANS 9:16 ESV

Father, sometimes I feel the need to get off the merry-go-round of life to rest for a time. The pace of this life will not let up; if I am waiting for a better time to take a day off or a less busy season to start that hobby I've been thinking about for months, that time won't ever come. Perhaps it's time to reconsider what my priorities look like.

The value of my life is not dependent on my output or intentions. You have already declared that I am enough in you. Why am I so easily convinced that meaning is wrapped up in what I do rather than in who I am? Your mercy covers me in my weakness and in my strength. Help me to lean into your heart, taking my cue for living from your wisdom and not from the expectations of the world.

God, I find my true value in you. As I look to you, I can see myself more clearly. Thank you for your wisdom that is always available. I want to live like you, not according to the expectations of my perfectionist views or of anyone else's beliefs about who I should be. I lean on you, God!

Close to Him

The LORD is near to all who call on him,
yes, to all who call on him in truth.

PSALM 145:18 NLT

When I feel isolated and alone, Father, the depths of the pain intensify. In my sadness, even calling a friend can feel like too much—if there's one that will answer me to begin with. But you are always there when I need you. You are closer than a brother; you are always at the ready to come to my rescue when I call on you.

Like a close, trusted friend, you can read between the lines. There is no need to pretend with you; I couldn't hide the true state of my heart from you even if I tried. There is no distance too great that you would not cover it. You close the gap between what I feel and the reality of your presence with the ease of your ready comfort. Help me to call to you in my dismay. You won't hesitate for a moment.

Lord, your nearness is my strength. You hold me up with the comfort of your presence. I need you today, God. Come and blow through the caverns of my soul. Bring light to the darkness within me and heal my wounds with the salve of your love. I am yours!

Accompanied by Love

Be strong and courageous. Do not be afraid or terrified because of them, for the LORD your God goes with you; he will never leave you nor forsake you.

DEUTERONOMY 31:6 NIV

God, when fear keeps me from moving forward, what should I do? Sometimes I succumb and talk myself out of whatever it is that lays on the other side of the fear. Other times I try to find another way around it. Your Word is full of statements that encourage me to take courage. I am not supposed to be afraid because I am unsure of what I am capable of; my strength lies in who goes with me—you!

I am not alone in my challenges, and I am not left to figure things out on my own. Where worry tries to convince me that I am not enough to keep going, faith says that although I can't work things out by myself, you are with me every step of the way, and you are able. You are all-knowing, all-powerful, and merciful, and you are my constant companion and confidant. I cannot lose when I am accompanied by you.

Lord, you are the champion of my heart. You have clear vision and endless wisdom, and I lean on you. When fear threatens my resolve, come closer and speak your words of life. Give me perspective to see your wonderful goodness with me every step of the way.

Goodness and Mercy

Oh, give thanks to the LORD, for He is good!
For His mercy endures forever.

1 CHRONICLES 16:34 NKJV

Father, when I look at the state of my life and I can only see what I am lacking, it is disheartening. The anxiety that rises with the unknowns of circumstances and the pain that I can't seem to escape feels like too much. If what you say is true, you are always good and your mercy goes on forever, so there must be some hope hiding within the lining of my life.

You are always with me. You never leave. You do not take days off and you don't move on to greener pastures. Wherever I am emotionally, physically, and mentally, you are with me. I am not too much for you to handle. You are not stumped by how to help me. You know exactly what I need. You are good. Your mercy is mine and I will see the fruit of your nearness in my life.

Merciful God, give me eyes to see where you are moving in my life right now. I yield my heart to you. I don't want to wallow in self-pity. I want—I need—to know your wisdom. Thank you for never leaving me. Come closer even now.

God of Justice

The LORD waits to be gracious to you,
and therefore he exalts himself to show mercy to you.
For the LORD is a God of justice;
blessed are all those who wait for him.

ISAIAH 30:18 ESV

Father, in the waiting, hope can feel like barely grasping a flimsy wish—like holding the string to a helium balloon that at any moment could float out of my grasp, never to be recovered. In reality, hope is more like roots going down into the soil; I cannot see how far they go, but they soak up the nutrients and cause growth above the ground. Hope that is rooted in the soil of your love cannot be lost.

God, you are not fickle; you are stable in mercy and steady in compassion. Your justice is better than any I've ever seen exemplified on this earth. Your pure motives qualify you to judge in an unbiased way. As I trust you, I will not be disappointed. Nothing goes wasted in your kingdom. I will find, in the end, that you pulled everything off perfectly.

Just One, you stand alone in wisdom and in love. Keep my heart entwined with yours that I wouldn't give up hope in your unfailing mercy. Keep me in the safety of your presence and fill me with your goodness. Give me the strength to keep walking with you.

Generations of Mercy

His mercy is for those who fear him
from generation to generation.

LUKE 1:50 NRSV

Father, whether I am a first-generation believer or I come from a long line of God-lovers, the fruit of families following you is full of mercy. As your child, I reap the benefits of those who have gone before me. You are as faithful today as you were yesterday. You are as devoted in this present age as you were in the days of Abraham, Moses, and David. Your character has not changed one iota.

Help me to humbly learn from those who have walked with you for longer than I have. As I share life with other God-lovers, I know that their faith will build my own. Help me to reflect on your goodness in my life and in the lives of those around me. I want to consider how your mercy has shaped me.

Faithful God, you never stop leaning in close with mercy. My life is yours. As I share my life with others who are going after you, I am encouraged by your faithfulness. You never stop loving, redeeming, and comforting. Thank you.

Great Kindness

Lord, answer me because your love is so good.
Because of your great kindness, turn to me.

PSALM 69:16 NCV

God, your response to me is never based on my own goodness. You do not require me to be a perfect example of holiness before you will help me. Thank goodness! You answer me out of the kindness of your heart. I am met by love at every turn. You will never meet me with anger, disappointment, or dismissal when I come to you in my humility or desperation.

You have shown me how you respond to repentance through the parable of the Prodigal Son. After the son had gone away from his father's house, squandered his inheritance, and lived out his rebellion, he was left with no options but to come back and beg for a place as a servant in his father's house. As soon as the father spotted his son approaching, he ran out to meet him, wrapped him in his own robe, restored his identity, and threw a huge celebration. This is the same love that meets me every time I come to you.

Kind Father, who else is like you in your tender mercy? I know that whenever I approach you, you come quickly, never hesitating in love. You are so good to me!

God's People

Once you were not a people,
but now you are God's people;
once you had not received mercy,
but now you have received mercy.

1 PETER 2:10 ESV

When I consider my life hidden with you, Jesus, the fruit is that I have been welcomed into a loving family where I am fully accepted. The mercy that covers me has imprinted me with your seal of approval. I belong to you. You will never shut me out or take away my rights as your child.

Sometimes I feel vulnerable in my place as your child. I feel like at any moment I could lose my position. Help me to recognize my place with you. I have been adopted into your inclusive family. No one can take my place and I can't lose my spot at your table of plenty. What is mine now is mine forever. I belong to you and you belong to me.

Good Father, I am so grateful to be your child. Encourage my heart today in your love; remind me what it means to be your own. I won't be tricked into believing that I don't belong anymore. You have said that I do, and your word is the only one that matters!

Compassion Overflowing

"Show mercy and compassion for others,
just as your heavenly Father overflows with mercy
and compassion for all."

LUKE 6:36 TPT

As I am met with love when I spend time in your presence,
God, I am filled to overflowing. What a wonderful
relationship I have with you, my kind God. Just as I am
shown mercy and compassion over and over again, may I
show the same kindness and forgiveness to others.

When I love others without condition or expecting any
benefit in return, I am reflecting your love that freely gives
to all without asking for anything. Even in this giving, I
have been filled by your power. Nothing that I give away
was mine to begin with. I am met with your kindness and
compassion every time I approach you. Every day is a new
opportunity to be filled up and poured out, ad infinitum!

Merciful Father, everything that you require is found
in what you freely offer. I cannot help but sing of your
goodness when I consider that you don't put conditions
on your love. May I love in the same way, constantly being
filled up to flow out to others.

To Be Known

I will be glad and rejoice in Your mercy,
For You have considered my trouble;
You have known my soul in adversities.

PSALM 31:7 NKJV

There is nothing within my life that is hidden from your sight, God. You see every detail: every question in my heart, every courageous act of faith, and the underlying beliefs that fuel my actions. You see my victories and you see my defeats. More than that, you come to my aid time and again, never leaving my side.

When life takes a drastic turn and the foundations that I thought were permanent begin to crumble, you are near. What can be shaken will be, but your faithfulness, love, and mercy will not be removed from my life. Just as you know me in every season of my soul, I will also see and know you in every high and low. When I look back over my life, the thread of your faithfulness will be clear to me.

Constant One, your presence is life to me in every season. Be near, Lord, even today. I need your perspective, wisdom, and grace.

My Savior

Guide me in your truth and teach me,
for you are God my Savior,
and my hope is in you all day long.

PSALM 25:5 NIV

When I don't know where to turn in the chaos of life, there is a sure place of comfort and safety waiting for me. When I take a break from trying to find solutions to the problems I face, I find rest in your arms, Father. Your presence is near and it is powerful.

Thank you that I don't have to do any more today to earn my place at your feast. I can lay down my burdens and find rest in you. You guide me in truth and teach me. I don't have to lay all the groundwork right now. When I am overwhelmed, it is the perfect time to take a moment to direct my attention to you and let you breathe life into me. You transmit your peace to me every time I ask for it.

Savior, you are my help all day long. When I stop and take a moment (or ten) to direct my gaze to you, I find that you meet me with love every time. You alone are my hope, God. No one else is like you.

Treasured Truth

Your laws are my treasure;
they are my heart's delight.

PSALM 119:111 NLT

Your laws, God, are full of your characteristic kindness
and mercy. You do not demand anything that you do not
give me the resources to live out. You lead me in your
unmatched wisdom on the pathway of life. You do not
guide me into destruction; everything you do is to build me
into a pillar of your love. You restore the wasted years and
rebuild the ruins that the storms of life left in their wake.

Your faithfulness is unparalleled. My heart will fill with
delight as I watch you work everything out for my good!
Where there is pain, you come with healing. Where there
is shame, you bring mercy that completely disarms it.
As I follow in your ways, I find that your nature is visible
everywhere I look. You are so worthy of my trust.

Good God, I follow you as you lead me on the path of your
pure love. Even in the trials, I know that your goodness will
prevail. You will lead me into life; of that, I'm sure. My heart
is yours, Lord. Continue to guide me.

Medicine for the Soul

A joyful, cheerful heart brings healing
to both body and soul.
But the one whose heart is crushed
struggles with sickness and depression.

PROVERBS 17:22 TPT

God, your nearness brings me joy unspeakable. Even in the valleys of deep despair, with you by my side, you are sowing peace into the paths I tread. When my heart is broken, you come in close as the comforter. I don't need to worry about the sadness that weighs me down. You meet me right in the middle of it and hold me. You carry me when I have no strength to move on my own.

Your joy is fortified within me in the constant connection I have in your presence. I am never disconnected from your heart. The relief I find in your nearness is a balm to my soul. You refuel my waning reserve of love. You meet me with the power of your compassion in every season. Help me to find the restoration my soul longs for in your nearness.

Holy One, your presence is full of joy. Heal my heart as you fill me with the power of your presence. I rely on you today and every day.

Met by Compassion

Blessed be the LORD!
For he has heard the voice of my pleas for mercy.

PSALM 28:6 ESV

When I don't know where to turn in my distress, and my heart feels completely sapped of all strength and hope, I turn to you, Father. You know me better than I know myself. Every time I call on you, you hear me and you meet me with mercy. There are no exceptions to your lavish love.

Thank you that you are not wearied by my requests. I don't have to rely on myself to figure a way out of my mess—there's no need to! I can lean into your love as I call on you. You will rush to meet me and give me the wisdom I so desperately need. You will not fail me. You make the impossible possible. I hand my difficult situations over to you because you can easily handle them.

Compassionate One, you are full of mercy every time I call out to you. I weary of my own requests, but I am reminded today that you never get tired of my voice. I won't hold anything back from you. I find relief in your presence.

Completely Covered

Amazingly, God—so full of compassion—
still forgave them.
He covered over their sins with his love,
refusing to destroy them all.
Over and over he held back his anger,
restraining wrath to show them mercy.

PSALM 78:38 TPT

God, your compassion is a well that will never run dry. You cannot be convinced out of your mercy or talked out of your love. You endlessly forgive; what a hope I've found! You always act in kindness because your heart is infinitely kind. Why would I stop myself from returning to you time and again when your love is better than life itself?

Father, when I consider your limitless love, my mind races with exceptions that I see in my life. But there are absolutely no exclusions to your love. Help me not to be tempted to disqualify myself because of my mistakes. I find as I submit to your love over and over again that it is sweeter each time.

God, what can I say about your love? It is almost incomprehensible that I am completely covered by your compassion every single moment of my life. Why would I hold myself back from you? I won't, Lord. Here I am! Cover me again in your unfailing love.

November

Be faithful to pray as intercessors
who are fully alert
and giving thanks to God.

COLOSSIANS 4:2 TPT

Held by Mercy

If I say, "My foot slips,"
Your mercy, O Lord, will hold me up.

PSALM 94:18 NKJV

When I consider the rising and setting of the sun, there is something even more predictable than this! I am met with mercy each time I come to you, God. It doesn't matter if I fail one time or a thousand, your response is always the same.

Sometimes I struggle to believe that you can forgive me when I repeatedly fail the expectations I set for myself. It is impossible to exhaust your tender love. You cannot be convinced out of your affection for me. Whether I find myself succeeding in life or struggling to get through the day, your kindness is always the same. I dare to hope that you are as good as you say you are. You will hold me up when I feel like I am falling.

Father of mercy, I won't keep myself from approaching you today. I have to hope that your goodness will not fail me. Even as I tremble at the thought of my own weakness, I ask that you would meet me with the power of your presence. Refine me and make me more like you. I won't stop coming back to you.

Alive in Mercy

Great is your mercy, O LORD;
give me life according to your justice.

PSALM 119:156 NRSV

I was created for so much more than just survival. Life is meant to be full of connection and growth. Where I lack, God, you fill me. You are the source of everything I need to thrive in this existence. In your life, I am made alive. Your presence within me is what empowers me to love others as you do.

I have been brought into fellowship with goodness itself. Your lavish mercy is unending and full of power to all who drink of its waters. I cannot fail when I am hemmed into your unfailing love. As the heavens are high above the earth, so your great love reaches farther than my grasp. Help me never lose interest in your heart of compassion that meets me with abundance.

Lord, you are greater than the highest mountain or the deepest sea. Your mysteries unfold before my eyes and I see glimpses of your goodness in every created thing. When I consider the beauty that is derived from darkness and pressure in the formation of diamonds, how could I question whether you are doing the same in me? Open my eyes to your wondrous ways.

Shine Light

Do everything without grumbling or arguing, so that you may become blameless and pure, "children of God without fault in a warped and crooked generation." Then you will shine among them like stars in the sky as you hold firmly to the word of life.

PHILIPPIANS 2:14-16 NIV

When I surrender my heart to you, Lord, I tether myself to your unfailing love. As I live in the place of submission, my life begins to reflect your perfect nature. In your light, I become light. I reflect your goodness when I am yielded to your kindness and mercy.

When my resources are running dry and I don't have much buffer of grace, help me to check my connection with you. When I don't spend enough time in your presence being filled by your love, I do not have what I need to give away. You are unending in your tender mercy. I come to you with my need again and again. It is not failure to need refreshing; unhindered connection is what I was designed for.

God, as your child, I come to you to be reminded of your good nature. I want to spend time in your presence, reawakening to the love that never ends and never changes. Only from this place of being filled up to overflowing can I freely give it away to others.

Alive Together

God, being rich in mercy, because of His great love with which He loved us, even when we were dead in our transgressions, made us alive together with Christ (by grace you have been saved).

EPHESIANS 2:4-5 NASB

Jesus, in areas of my life where I see destruction and devastation, there is hope. I have been made alive with you in your resurrection. This means that whatever doesn't look fruitful is awaiting your redemption. There is no situation too bleak that you cannot bring beauty and regeneration from it.

You are in the business of doing the impossible. What seems out of the question in my mind is an invitation to faith and trust in your miracle-working power. I have been covered in grace that empowers me. You change me from the inside out and bring beauty out of the ashes of despair. And you do it again and again! Help me to put my hope in you, for you are surely not finished with me yet.

God, you are so rich in mercy. It is almost incomprehensible that I cannot deplete your love in my life. Thank you for a reality that is more wonderful than my highest hopes. Breathe on the barren parts of my life and heart and bring new life as only you can do.

Persistent Peace

The Lord will fight for you,
and you shall hold your peace.

Exodus 14:14 NKJV

When situations spiral out of my control and I can't see the way out, God, you are my firm foundation. You do not change with the shifting winds that send my mind spinning. In you I find my peace, and it's the kind that can't be taken from me. You will fight the battles that I cannot; when I rely on you, I will see that you executed everything perfectly.

Even in the midst of troubles and storms, you are unchanging and I am hidden in you. If you are not shaken, neither will I be. You are my refuge and strength, and you will not let me be crushed by the weight of my burdens. You fight for me! You will never stop defending me as long as it is called today.

Lord, fight for me. You see the areas that are completely out of my depth and control; there's nothing I can do to help myself. You are so much wiser than I am. You see it all from the beginning to the end and everything in between. Fill my heart with peace and confidence as I rest in your unfailing love.

Return

Let the wicked forsake their way,
and the unrighteous their thoughts;
let them return to the Lord,
that he may have mercy on them,
and to our God,
for he will abundantly pardon.

ISAIAH 55:7 NRSV

God, you are a gracious Father. You patiently wait for me to return to you when I insist on going my own way. When I am lost to my own whims and desires, I find that nothing is enough to satisfy the longing of relationship I have for you. In you I have all the goodness I am looking for.

I don't want to find pleasure and fulfillment my own way. There is no time limit to your mercy. Today is the perfect opportunity to return to you, my good Father. You always welcome me with open arms when I approach you. I don't need to be afraid of your judgment; you are full of love and forgiveness, and you will restore everything back to me. It is not too good to be true—it is your promise to me.

Merciful Father, I can't begin to thank you for all that you've done for me. Even in my wandering, you love me. I come back to you with my heart wide open. What a relief that you receive me and wash me clean in your love. I am undone in your presence.

Wonderful Grace

His unforgettable works of surpassing wonder
reveal his grace and tender mercy.

PSALM 111:4 TPT

Sometimes when I am holding onto hope, I reduce your incredible mercy to lofty ideals, Father. The reality of your goodness is that you tangibly work amazing things in my life. Where I struggle to see your kindness at work in my life right now, help me to press into your presence until I see through your eyes of love.

God, you are a miracle worker. You do what no one else could dream of doing. If there are circumstances in my life that oppose your compassion, I can be sure that restoration is coming. You specialize in redemption, and you never give up in love. You are not done with me yet.

Good God, you are more loving than I can imagine. Holy Spirit, meet me in the midst of both my messes and my joys today. I don't want a single moment to go wasted, knowing that you are always working. Entwine my heart with yours so I sense you in everything. Don't stop working in wonderful ways.

Lasting Virtues

Three things will last forever—
faith, hope, and love—
and the greatest of these is love.

1 Corinthians 13:13 NLT

Father, when everything else fades away in life, there are three things that remain unchanged: confident trust based on your good character and faithfulness, hopeful expectation of the fulfillment of your promises, and love that conquers all fears.

Your love is greater than any other force known in the heavens or on the earth. It is strong enough to defeat death, powerful enough to make the sick well, and faithful enough to cover every living thing that has ever existed. Where I have been limited in love, I pray that your mercy would meet me in new ways that blow open every box that I put it in. Where I have put boundaries on kindness, let me see today that this is not what you do. Your compassion is wider reaching than I could ever comprehend.

Loving God, you are wealthy in love in ways that I try but fail to imagine. Make your mercy more real to me today as I look for you everywhere I go. Give me eyes to see a glimpse of the limitless love you pour out on all. I know that you are better than I give you credit for.

Leaning In

Hear the voice of my pleas for mercy,
when I cry to you for help,
when I lift up my hands
toward your most holy sanctuary.

PSALM 28:2 ESV

When I am in need, it is not a fault, God. Self-sufficiency is not a fruit of your Spirit, nor is it a requirement of worth. In fact, I find my true identity wrapped up in your love that never changes and has nothing to do with my circumstances. When I cry out to you, you hear and answer.

I admit I feel like a failure when I recognize areas in my life that are lacking. Today I align myself with your perspective. I boldly come to you, asking for everything I need with an unfiltered heart. You won't let me down, and you won't leave me the same. I lean into your tender love.

Good Father, here I am coming to you again. I won't try to dress myself up today or pretend that I'm not hurting. You see my heart so clearly; why do I try to hide from you? Meet me with the power of your mercy that changes me. I rely on you, Lord.

Like Minded

Rejoice, be made complete, be comforted,
be like-minded, live in peace;
and the God of love and peace will be with you.

2 Corinthians 13:11 nasb

When I live in isolation, God, everything feels more concentrated. Sadness has nowhere to go but to steep in my soul, and I must rely on my own reserves to get by. The problem with this is that I was never meant to go it alone. A shared burden is less heavy, and comfort from a friend is priceless.

When I find people I can trust, it takes practice to remain vulnerable enough to share the realities of my hardships. It is important to have people who are leaning into faith with me; together we become like iron, sharpening each other as we live with openness. I will experience you in even deeper ways as I share life with others who are also leaning into your love.

Father, I see that you have created me for community. Where I am isolated, would you provide safe people with whom I can grow? I don't want to live relying solely on my own strength and resources. I know that I live a limited life if it is not in connection with others. Help me to see how I can be more open.

Kind God

May the LORD show you his kindness
and have mercy on you.

NUMBERS 6:25 NCV

In most religions, gods are not known for their kindness. They are known for power and impossible requirements. But you are the Lord of all of heaven and earth, and you stand above the rest. You are full of mercy and power. Your compassion dictates your interactions with me. You do not require me to be or do anything good on my own. What kind of a God is that?

In goodness, you show me the tender affections of your heart through the faithfulness of your presence with me. You are not easily angered, and you do not grow impatient with me even though I deserve it by my own standards. You are so much greater. Your ways are higher than mine and your motives purer than my best intentions. Help my heart to know the fullness of your kindness toward me and never lose hope.

God of kindness, you are so much better than I could ever dream of being. I'm so grateful that you are patient in love and full of mercy toward me every single day. Just when I feel like I have exhausted your goodness, you remind me that you are the same yesterday, today, and forever. Show me your love again, Lord!

No More Walls

He himself is our peace,
who has made us both one
and has broken down in his flesh
the dividing wall of hostility.

EPHESIANS 2:14 ESV

Restoration of connection with you, Father, has been given to me freely through the sacrifice and power of Jesus' resurrection. Where there was once a wall of hostility raised in my heart, there is now an openness of relationship. There is nothing that holds me back. Jesus broke down every obstacle that once kept me from knowing you in the fullness of fellowship.

God, if there is any hostility left in my heart, I ask you to expose it. There is nothing that can stand against your strong love; you yourself have done the hard work of restoration. Please show me if there is any hesitation in my heart toward you. I ask your presence to bring light to the source of it.

God of peace, you are so rich in love and mercy. I don't want to resist your love in any area of my life, so lead me into healing and restoration where I lack understanding. I believe that you are better to me than I am to myself. I trust you!

Perfect Peace

"Peace I leave with you; my peace I give to you.
I do not give to you as the world gives.
Do not let your hearts be troubled,
and do not let them be afraid."

JOHN 14:27 NRSV

When fear threatens to send me running from reality, help me to take a moment to breathe in your very-present nearness, Father. You have not left me to my own survival skills and coping mechanisms. There is a better way. Your peace is like a warm, fragrant breeze in the springtime. It fills me with the awareness of the here and now and the sweetness of the fragrant presence of what is close by. Though I cannot see your Spirit, I know the ways in which he moves.

You do not give like those expecting something in return. Freely you give; freely let me receive. Peace that transcends my understanding is the peace you give; it meets me in confusion and brings clarity. It calms my restless heart and brings relief to the stresses that would keep me on edge. God, you are so good, and your love is more predictable than fear.

Steady One, you are perfect in power, love, and peace. I need you to calm my anxieties and breathe your peace into my body. May I align with the stability of your kindness today. I am yours. Fill me with your peace.

Filled to Overflowing

Look at how much encouragement you've found in your relationship with the Anointed One! You are filled to overflowing with his comforting love. You have experienced a deepening friendship with the Holy Spirit and have felt his tender affection and mercy.

PHILIPPIANS 2:1 TPT

When I submit my life to you, God, it is not like a servant yielding to a master. It is more like a child trusting a caring parent. You are full of mercy and love, an ever-present help in times of trouble, and you are full of joyful delight in me.

Your comforting love meets me when I need it most. It is an ever-flowing fountain of compassion that does not stop covering me. In friendship with you, I feel your kindness and tender care. What an amazing relationship! Where others leave me feeling unsatisfied, I find ultimate fulfillment in your love that always heals, always restores, and always draws me in.

God of abundance, you are the source of everything good. Your presence awakens me to life over and over again. I am not just filled with enough but filled to overflowing. Do it again, Lord!

Ours in Christ

Grace, mercy and peace will be with us,
from God the Father and from Jesus Christ,
the Son of the Father, in truth and love.

2 JOHN 1:3 NASB

As I walk this earth, God, I face trials and troubles of many kinds. I can't escape pain, and I can't ignore suffering. It is not a gift of your Spirit to deny the ache of the hurting. This is not how you operate. You are quick to comfort, patient in mercy, and full of kindness to the heartbroken.

I need your grace to meet me today. I need your peace to flood my life. I need your mercy for so many things. Thank you that you meet me with the abundance of your heart. You freely give all that I need. I boldly ask you to fill me today; you will not let me down.

Jesus Christ, in you is all truth and love. I will not hold back from you today. Here is my heart, in its laid-bare state just as it is. Come and meet me with the power of your presence and revive me.

Glory Coming

He will take our weak mortal bodies and change them into glorious bodies like his own, using the same power with which he will bring everything under his control.

PHILIPPIANS 3:21 NLT

There is no escaping the mortality of my body, Father. Thankfully, my ultimate hope is not in my health in this life. When sickness saps my strength and steals my ambition, it can be difficult to adjust my mind. You are my healer, and that is true in every age. Even when you don't heal, you are still as good as you ever were.

The fundamental confident expectation of my faith is that you will raise me to everlasting life just as Jesus was raised with a glorified body no longer confined to the mortality of his limited form. I will be changed, once and for all, in your power in the resurrection of my body. Whether I am weak or strong now, I will one day be faultless in every way. What a glorious hope.

Holy One, my firm hope is in the coming glory of eternity with you. I know that life now is full of ups and downs, victories and failures, but with you by my side, I can face it all. You empower me to live with hope, and even when that falters, I know that you will never fail.

Set on the Spirit

To set the mind on the flesh is death,
but to set the mind on the Spirit is life and peace.

ROMANS 8:6 ESV

God, when the worries of life overtake my mind, finding peace within it seems impossible. Despair is not far behind the anxieties that send me spiraling. When I focus on the lack of my circumstances, I feel as if there is no way out, and the desperation to try and do everything I can to fix it further depletes my emotional resources.

But there is another way! When I consider the Holy Spirit and the fruit that he so freely gives, I align myself with hope and faith. Help me not to be drawn into the spiral of unmet needs; rather, help me look to your unchanging character. Your faithfulness is steady and sure, and I will see your goodness. I have seen you come through for me again and again.

Ever-present One, thank you for not leaving me to the downward spiral of my anxiety. Holy Spirit, I need you. As I set my heart and thoughts on you, let hope rise again. Breathe peace into my worried heart as I direct my gaze to you. Your faithfulness is sure and you will not let me down. I believe it, Lord.

Led into Truth

"When he, the Spirit of truth, comes,
he will guide you into all the truth."

JOHN 16:13 NIV

Jesus, when you ascended into heaven, you did not leave us alone. In fact, you clearly told your disciples that it was better that you go so that your Spirit could come and minister to all. The Spirit is not confined to a human body, space, or time. He moves freely and widely, dwelling with me in every moment in very tangible ways.

Holy Spirit, you illuminate the truth. You lead me into wisdom. When I am clouded by doubt and confusion, you bring clarity. What an amazing reality that I have the same Spirit alive in me that raised Jesus from the dead! Your power, wisdom, and compassion are unrivaled, and you freely give to all who ask. Help me to continue to invite you into my life. You are tangible love and wisdom.

Wise One, you lead me along the path of truth. When I start to wander, you bring me back to your love time and again. Don't stop doing it, Holy Spirit. I rely on you for everything I need. You see it all. Meet me where I am and lead me on.

No Wandering

I have tried hard to find you—
don't let me wander from your commands.

PSALM 119:10 NLT

God, your abundant grace is always mine in the same measure. It doesn't matter if I've followed you my whole life or for one year. As I walk down your path of love, I find that when I begin to wander, you gently redirect me.

How can I know if I am wandering from your ways? I know it has nothing to do with my bank account, the state of my health, or the success of my career. Help me to look within. What do my thoughts look like? What is the attitude of my heart on most days? Am I quick to judge? Do I feel worthless in love and life? These would be indicators that I need a realignment in your love. Meet me with the abundance of your heart today.

Merciful God, I submit my heart to yours again today. Where I am depleted of compassion, fill me with the kindness of your heart. I cannot continue to choose love in my own strength, but I know that you empower me as you freely fill me with your mercy. Thank you, God.

Persistent Grace

In Your great mercy You did not
utterly consume them nor forsake them;
For You are God, gracious and merciful.

NEHEMIAH 9:31 NKJV

God, when I encounter your amazing mercy in my life, I cannot deny your goodness. I have heard of your great compassion before, but until I experienced it for myself, it simply sounded like a nice idea. I was made for relationship and knowing you has never been about intellectually consuming philosophies. I am a whole being with real needs that you meet with your very real provisions.

Your presence is made manifest in the Holy Spirit, and the Spirit ministers to all who call on the name of the Lord. This includes me! When I struggle to experience your love beyond the confines of my mind, I invite you to minister to my heart with your tangible presence. You will fill, empower, and graciously meet me. My entire being was always meant to be wholly brought into fellowship with you.

God, you are full of grace to all who look for it. In the power of your presence, meet me today with more than the changing of thoughts. Fill my entire being with your love. I want to know the tangible power of your presence in my life.

But God

I had said in my alarm,
"I am cut off from your sight."
But you heard the voice of my pleas for mercy
when I cried to you for help.

PSALM 31:22 ESV

When all seems to be right in my little world and the sun is shining bright, it is easy to recognize your blessing and favor, Lord. In circumstances where I can't escape the suffering and pain that life sends my way, it is almost second nature to question how you could change so drastically. However, the Word is clear that you are unchanging in love and mercy. Your tender kindness is never uncertain.

When I am faced with tragedy, does it influence my view of you? Do I think that somehow you have forgotten me? You never waver in compassion, and your thoughts toward me are full of delight in who I am no matter the circumstance. Where my experiences are not matching up with your character, help me to cry out for your goodness to break through. You will never leave me hanging; your mercy meets me at every juncture.

Lord, you are never changing in your perfect nature. When I am struggling to see your goodness at work in my life, come close and fill me with your perspective. Give me the peace of your presence and the mercy of your heart. I rely on you today and forever.

At Peace

If while we were still enemies, God fully reconciled us to himself through the death of his Son, then something greater than friendship is ours. Now that we are at peace with God, and because we share in his resurrection life, how much more we will be rescued from sin's dominion!

ROMANS 5:10 TPT

God, your peace is so much richer than the temporary calm I feel when all seems to be right with the world. Your peace reaches into the chaos and brings order. It speaks to the storms that are raging and brings complete tranquility. Even when seas still churn around me, you give me stillness and clarity within.

I can never earn your acceptance or love; it is mine. It always has been! Your intentions are full of goodness, love, and mercy. Your joy is unrivaled, meeting me when I need it most. I am not just counted as your friend but as your own child; I am a part of your everlasting kingdom. When my heart begins to falter, I ask that your resurrection power would raise me back to life.

Great God, your peace is unlike anything I've experienced. It brings clarity of mind and wisdom even in the harshest of circumstances. It stills the chaos of my mind and fills my body with rest. I am safe in your constant love, and this is my portion forever. Come near, Lord, in the peace of your presence.

Spirit Powered

May the God of hope fill you with all joy and peace in believing, so that you will abound in hope by the power of the Holy Spirit.

ROMANS 15:13 NASB

Joy is not a side effect of normal living at the pace this world is going, God. Peace is not a natural reaction to the chaos that is everywhere. These values are both cultivated and given through fellowship with you. The more time I spend in your presence, the more peace and joy become a part of the fabric of my being. I learn what it is to walk in love with hope as my vision.

You are the source of every good thing. Fill me with everything I need to believe. Your faithfulness will supply every necessity. Help me not to hesitate to press into your presence every time I remember to. You do not disappoint and you won't ever grow tired of my attention.

Ever-present One, you are as vital to me as the air in my lungs. I rely on you for more than strength to go on, but for every good thing in this life. Your joy is unmatched and your peace is beyond comprehension. You are so, so good. Envelop me in your love again today as I rest in you.

Abundantly Blessed

God is able to bless you abundantly,
so that in all things at all times,
having all that you need,
you will abound in every good work.

2 Corinthians 9:8 niv

Thank you, God, that I am not destined to a life of "just enough." I was never meant to struggle to get by, and you do not give like a stingy old miser. There is always room for more, both in the asking and the receiving. Whatever season of life I am in, your abilities are always bigger than my own. Will I choose to trust you?

Thank you for the areas in my life that are going well. For those places where I'm struggling, I ask you to move in power and work on me. Your strength is made perfect in my weakness. You have wise strategies that will transform even the bleakest situation. I want to spend time in your presence today so I am filled with your abundant love and mercy that changes me from the inside out.

Provider, you are rich in mercy and lovingkindness. Out of the abundance of your heart you give to all who have need. See my needs, Lord. They are plain before you. I won't stop asking for your hand of goodness to be on my life so I may run after you all of my days.

A Better Way

Judgment will be without mercy
to anyone who has shown no mercy;
mercy triumphs over judgment.

JAMES 2:13 NRSV

Mercy is the way of the cross. When I follow you, Jesus, I see there is no other way to live like you unless I am choosing to continually live in love. That sounds easy, but it is for sure the more costly way. When I lay down my life in love, I forgive instead of seeking revenge, I am kind to those who ridicule me, and I sacrifice my own comfort for the truth.

Love is not some flighty ideal but a grounded surrendering. But it is the better way! Your Word says that I will be judged according to how I judge. This brings me pause. Am I living with mercy as my covering, or am I keeping love at a distance by judging others continuously?

Merciful God, you are the way, the truth, and the life. As I live in your example, I will find the fullness of my life is in you. Help me to choose kindness instead of harsh criticism. May my heart remain humble in your love as I learn to let go of my own hurt and rejection.

Confident Approach

Let us then with confidence draw near to the throne of grace, that we may receive mercy and find grace to help in time of need.

HEBREWS 4:16 ESV

In your family, God, there are no black sheep. Your love is pure and welcoming to each in the same measure of abundant tenderness. I have been welcomed into your family, so there is no reason to hesitate to come to you. You will not ridicule my questions or brush off my pain. You are perfect in compassion and love that satisfies every condition of my soul.

I want to learn to boldly approach you. I want to come to you with confidence, not cautiously circling your table of plenty. I am not supposed to pick up the crumbs of others' portions. There is a place reserved for me with everything that will satisfy me piled high, waiting for me to take my place.

Good Father, I will not hesitate to approach your throne of grace today. Here I come, all of me, trusting that you will receive me just as I am. Here at your table of plenty I will eat until I am satisfied. Give me everything I need for the day and more. You are the only one who turns ashes into beauty, and I trust you!

He Is Better

To the LORD our God belong mercy and forgiveness,
though we have rebelled against Him.

DANIEL 9:9 NKJV

God, you are full of forgiveness. That is a statement that could be meditated on every day for the rest of my life, and I still wouldn't reach the end of its power or significance. You are not a one-time giver of mercy. You do not have a limit to your love, and you don't have a threshold to your forgiveness. I cannot weary you with my failures. Even if I could, you would still choose to show me kindness.

The world does not know this kind of generous love. It is a foreign concept to most. Even when I am yielded to your great compassion, am I not surprised by the depths of your mercy time and again? I could never reach the end of it; what a glorious mystery. May the eyes of my heart be enlightened to see you as you are today—perfect in love, power, and full of glory!

God, your love is better than anything I've ever known. It never withdraws, always flows toward me, and lifts me up every time I fall. Though I frequently disappoint myself, I find time and again that I haven't disappointed you which is a marvelous mystery. Fill me with the light of your love again today.

Profound Wisdom

If you are truly wise,
you'll learn from what I've told you.
It's time for you to consider these profound lessons
of God's great love and mercy.

PSALM 107:43 TPT

When I was growing up, I learned from trial and error, but I also learned by following the example of trusted people in my life. True wisdom is found in following your pure example of mercy, God. It's a sure bet that when I align my life with your unfailing love, I will be found in you.

When I spend time in your presence, I cannot help but soak up your goodness. I reflect the nature of those I spend most of my time with. What am I filling my time with? Even in the background of my life, what I give my attention to is what feeds my thoughts and heart. Help me to be thoughtful in my time and intentional with what I consume.

God, when I look back over my life and see what you have done, I am amazed. There is no end to your kindness and tender mercy. As I remember who you have been, meet me in this present moment and do a new thing. You are rich in love, and I am rich in you.

God's Mouthpiece

The LORD reached out his hand and touched my mouth
and said to me, "I have put my words in your mouth."

JEREMIAH 1:9 NIV

Words matter. Anyone in relationship knows that this is
true. Words can build up or they can tear down. Am I
purposeful in the words I choose, God? Do I consider what
I will say before I speak, especially in times of vulnerability,
or do I let words spill from the overflow of my mind and
heart in instant reaction?

When I submit my life to you, it should include my mind
and mouth. I won't always get it right, and that's where
mercy comes in. When my speech is peace-loving and
courageously honest while maintaining compassion, I know
that I am reflecting your character in my approach. I show
your nature when I choose humility, mercy, and kindness.
Help me to reflect you in this way.

Lord, touch my lips and make me clean. I know that as I
spend time with you, relating to you in your unmatched
mercy, that I won't be able to stop myself from showing
your nature. And when I don't, I will walk in the way of
humility, asking for forgiveness. Fill me that I may pour out
to others.

Empowered

May he give you the power to accomplish
all the good things your faith prompts you to do.

2 Thessalonians 1:11 NLT

When I am full of faith, my intentions are set high on
being a living sacrifice for you, God. When I feel good, it
is so much easier to say, "Yes, Lord!" with a willing heart.
When my realities shift and suffering lasts for longer than
expected, what then? Do I give up and decide that I am
disqualified? Or do I keep persevering in faith even when it
feels impossible and, perhaps, pointless?

Thankfully, the requirement of faithfully following you
is not my own stamina or ability. Perseverance is found
in continuing to choose to press into you even (and
especially) when I feel completely weak and unworthy.
Holy Spirit, you are my source for strength. You empower
me to keep going, and you will fill me with all that I need to
not just survive but to thrive. Help me to turn my attention
to you today and be filled afresh.

Holy Spirit, you are the source of everything I need. I yield
my heart to yours, knowing that your unfailing love meets
me at every single turn. Invade the moments of my day
with your tangible grace that strengthens me to do all that
you would have me do.

December

The LORD is close to everyone
who prays to him,
to all who truly pray to him.

PSALM 145:18 NCV

Invited

> "Now you should go and study the meaning of the verse: I want you to show mercy, not just offer me a sacrifice. For I have come to invite the outcasts of society and sinners, not those who think they are already on the right path."
>
> MATTHEW 9:13 TPT

Jesus, you were a perfect reflection of the heart of your Father. When you invited the sick, weak, and broken into your sphere, you clearly showed that God welcomes in those who the world shuts out. There are no outcasts in your kingdom, only members of the same family, all with the same dignity and worth.

Whether I feel acceptable or not within society, God, you are for me. It does not matter if I measure up to the world's standards. You welcome me with the love of a tender father. Your compassionate heart is turned toward me in affection. Help me to lay down my defenses and come to you, you are waiting to receive me with open arms.

God, I come to you with an open heart looking for belonging. I know that I will find it in you. Meet me with the power of your love that calms every fear. I am covered in your mercy.

Kept in Love

Keep yourselves in the love of God,
waiting for the mercy of our Lord Jesus Christ
that leads to eternal life.

JUDE 1:21 ESV

In the chaos of this world, it can be difficult to remain at peace, Father. There are endless things competing for my attention; how do I rein it all in and focus my thoughts on what matters most? If the threat of anxiety is a constant battle, there are surely areas in my life that need reprioritizing.

When I am kept in your mercy that surrounds me, my fears are calmed. Your presence envelops me with love and I find the stillness of confidence that leads me to rest. When the pace of life just won't quit, help me to practice slowing down and setting boundaries on my time and attention. As I do this, even the mundane feels more meaningful.

Loving God, you constantly surround me with the embrace of your compassion. Do not leave me to my own whims, Lord. I want to find rest in the peace of your presence. Teach me as I take steps to walk in wisdom.

Strength to Stand

Your words have comforted those who fell,
and you have strengthened
those who could not stand.

JOB 4:4 NCV

God, you are a support to the weak and strength to the wavering. You never require me to rely on my own abilities in life, not even on my best days. In my frailty, your power is perfectly shown off. I can never veer too far off the path of your love that you cannot bring me back. I am kept in love even when I wander.

When sorrow saps every emotional reserve I have, I can't even stand on my own. In these moments, Comforter, you come closer than I've known and you camp in the battlefield of my heart. You bind the broken parts and tend to the wounds. You leave no part untouched by your unfailing love. You make a dwelling place within me and you do your restorative work.

God of my comfort, come close with your presence. You don't require me to stand or to do anything. You meet me in my pain and suffering and you go to work healing and tending to me. You are too wonderful for words. Don't ever stop your beautiful work in my heart.

Increased Honor

You will increase my honor,
and comfort me once again.

PSALM 71:21 NRSV

My worth is found in you, God, the one who has given me life. I don't need to earn even a portion of my honor. You freely offer dignity to all, not missing anyone. What a tremendous relief it is that you are the giver of my inherent worth. You are kind in nature, merciful, and forever compassionate, and you esteem me as your child. With a father like that, I could never lose my dignity to another; even if I did, you would restore it.

You give me my value and you increase my honor. With my life woven into yours, I cannot help but reflect the goodness of your nature. You are perfectly peaceful and wonderfully kind. Help me not to lose heart when I falter or fail, for even then I am covered by your mercy.

Lord, you are the lifter of my head and my firm foundation. I find my true identity wrapped up in your presence; in your light, I see more clearly. Thank you for loving me. I cannot begin to deserve your endless kindness toward me.

Sing for Joy

Sing for joy, O heavens, and exult, O earth;
break forth, O mountains, into singing!
For the Lord has comforted his people,
and will have compassion on his suffering one.

ISAIAH 49:13 NRSV

When I am under the weight of suffocating circumstances that don't seem to change as I cry out for help, God, comfort me and lift the weight of the burden. Your compassion is not absent from anything I go through. Draw near in kindness and bring peace with your presence.

The birds cannot stop singing, and the winds have their own song. Why would I hold mine back when your mercy is clearly at hand? Let me lift my songs to you: in rejoicing, in surrender, in awe, and in the waiting. You are always worthy! Though I change, you never do.

God, you are always worthy of the praise I offer you, yet you don't demand it from me. You are kind in your patience. What a wonderful God you are. I present my heart to you today, and I lift my voice as an offering of gratitude. You are so, so good!

Ready Relief

You who are my Comforter in sorrow,
my heart is faint within me.

JEREMIAH 8:18 NIV

God of the angel armies, you war on behalf of the vulnerable. You are the same God who draws close to the brokenhearted. You lift the burdens of the weary and carry the weak into places of rest. You have never turned away from a wounded soul looking for reprieve. You are the strength that brings respite to the tired and liberation to the tied down.

My heart needs relief today. Draw close to me in my place of need. You never miss the mark. Your unfailing love floods my heart, mind, and body. You satisfy with your mercy, and you won't leave me wanting. God, where I am looking for help, please answer me quickly and clearly in your wisdom.

Comforter, in your arms I find the relief I am looking for. Your love ministers to my heart in ways that I can't even put into words. Thank you for your mercy that never leaves me. I rely on you for the wisdom I need. Come in power again.

Thread of Faithfulness

My loving God, the harp in my heart will praise you.
Your faithful heart toward us
will be the theme of my song.
Melodies and music will rise to you,
the Holy One of Israel.

PSALM 71:22 TPT

Everything you do is done with faithfulness as the thread holding it all together, God. You create a tapestry out of the cords of my life. What you do is beautiful and far beyond my understanding. Your love is stitched into the fabric of my life. When I look back, I see that you have been working all along. There is no place that your redemption leaves untouched.

When I look back over my life, I see your love at work even when I was completely unaware of it at the time. I see your fingerprints on my story. Where I struggle to see you, I pause for a moment to ask for your perspective. Show me where you were. You are so faithful to answer me.

Loving God, your faithfulness is woven into my life. Give me eyes to see where you were in areas I thought were untouched by you. I submit my heart to yours, knowing that you are kind, gentle, and for me. Speak, Lord.

Weary Comforted

The Sovereign LORD has given me his words of wisdom,
so that I know how to comfort the weary.
Morning by morning he wakens me
and opens my understanding to his will.

ISAIAH 50:4 NLT

God, your wisdom is given for all to understand. Those who seek your guidance will find it; your perfect nature does not go back on any of your promises. Those who seek you will find you; those who mourn will be comforted. Those who hope in you will not be disappointed. What a wonderful God you are!

As I spend time in your Word and in your presence, you give me the revelation light of understanding that opens my heart and mind to your perfect ways. The length of your love no one can fathom. There is no beginning and no end to your mercy. May my heart grow in confidence of your perfect love as I soak it in more and more every day.

Holy One, you offer unending kindness to those who come to you. Fill me with the understanding of your goodness and your wonderful character as I look to you. There is no one else like you.

Never Left

"Blessed are the poor in spirit,
for theirs is the kingdom of heaven.
Blessed are those who mourn,
for they will be comforted."

MATTHEW 5:3-4 NIV

God, you are a constant source of comfort in the midst of my suffering. You do not leave me in my pain, and you certainly do not turn away from me in my desperation. You are always with me. You comfort the mourning, strengthen the weak, and offer hope to the heartbroken. Your love never fails.

How can I begin to understand what it means that you will never abandon me? No matter what I'm facing, you are with me in every moment. Right where I am, in whatever circumstance I am up against, you are there. Thank you for being near.

God of all comfort, I cling to you today. Even when my voice cracks and I can't form words, there you are in complete understanding. Holy Spirit, come closer as I turn my attention to you.

Father of Mercies

Blessed be the God and Father of our Lord Jesus Christ, the Father of mercies and God of all comfort, who comforts us in all our affliction so that we will be able to comfort those who are in any affliction with the comfort with which we ourselves are comforted by God.

2 CORINTHIANS 1:3-4 NASB

When I am overcome by the burdens of life, there is someone I can turn to who is closer than a brother. God, my Father of all mercy and the greatest comforter, you are a safe place I can run into. There is no better friend.

Every struggle and every sorrow I experience is a place where you offer relief and consolation. There is no burden too big that you stay away. There is nothing that intimidates you, and there is no shame too heavy that you will not lift it. As I am comforted by your tender care, I am able to offer this same kind of comfort to others.

Father, you are faithful in lovingkindness. Your tenderness is reassuring to my weary soul. When I can barely stand, you hold me. Thank you for never leaving me; your constant presence is life to me.

Unbiased God

The LORD wants to show his mercy to you.
He wants to rise and comfort you.
The LORD is a fair God,
and everyone who waits
for his help will be happy.

ISAIAH 30:18 NCV

God, your love cannot be exhausted by my questioning.
Your patience is much longer than mine. You welcome me
even with my hesitations about your character. My doubts
won't last long in your presence, but even if they did, they
would not diminish your power.

Your love welcomes everyone with the openness of your
eager heart. You do not give in one measure to some and
to others more or less. You give equally to all. When I wait
for your help, I will not be disappointed. You comfort me
as I rest in you. Your nearness is so rich. I can't help but be
loved to life by you over and over again.

Lord, you are amazing in your unbiased nature. I'm thankful
that you don't look at me the way the world does. You see
each person as worthy of your unending love. I am worthy
of love because you have said that I am. I lean into your
heart again today.

Born into Hope

All you who put your hope in the LORD
be strong and brave.

PSALM 31:24 NCV

When I am lacking in hope, where do I go to find perspective, Jesus? Spending too much time focused on my troubles can cause anxiety to rise as I consider my lack of options. But you are full of miracle-working power; you also have much clearer perspective than I do.

In you I have a hope that cannot be diminished. You have given me new life in your resurrection power. I no longer need to fear death or its consequences. There is so much anticipation in the glory that awaits me. Eternal life without pain, suffering, or limitations is mine through you. You are forever kind, full of mercy, and you cover me in compassion—both now and forever.

Jesus, you are the hope that I cling to in the long days of waiting. There is no one as wonderful as you. I am so grateful to have been born into your kingdom. Thank you for mercy that covers me every moment of my life. Awaken my heart to the hope I have in you.

Sincere Wisdom

The wisdom from above is first pure, then peaceable, gentle, open to reason, full of mercy and good fruits, impartial and sincere.

JAMES 3:17 ESV

Your wisdom, God, is full of pure motives. You do not have a hidden agenda. Wisdom is peace-loving and gentle, causing me to consider a better way. There is kindness inherent in the revelation that you give; the fruit of it cannot be mistaken. It is genuine and unbiased, not being easily swayed. Your perfect nature is evident in the wisdom that you give in your Word.

When I am looking for guidance, help me to turn to you. I know that your advice is the only kind I can fully trust. I submit my plans to you and you direct me. I know that wisdom is guiding me when it is full of the characteristics of your nature. I don't need to overcomplicate it; you are faithful to help me.

Wise One, you are the source of every answer I'm looking for. I know that you won't disappoint me as I follow you. I need you more than I know how to express. Fill me with your love as I surrender my mind to you today.

Better than Sacrifice

I desire mercy and not sacrifice,
And the knowledge of God
more than burnt offerings.

HOSEA 6:6 NKJV

God, your requirements are vastly different than the demands I place on myself. In a world of endless to-do lists, I am constantly fighting the strain that this kind of pace requires. When I push to require more of myself and others, you encourage mercy. Compassion is your way.

When I approach you, help me not to come with all of my accomplishments in my back pocket, ready to let you know what I'm doing for you. I want to come to you with a humble heart longing for connection. You never turn away a hungry heart; doing great things for you isn't the point of relationship with you. It is not worthless, but it is not where I find my worth.

Merciful God, I know that in knowing you, I will become more like you. Help me to be as gracious with myself as you are. Give me a tender heart for those around me as well, so I have compassion for them instead of criticism. Your way of mercy is so much better than my way of storing up achievements.

Show Me

Magnify the marvels of your mercy to all who seek you.
Make your Pure One wonderful to me,
like you do for all those who turn aside
to hide themselves in you.

PSALM 17:7 TPT

There is no safer place to find myself than in your heart,
God When I hide myself in you, your beauty surrounds me.
Your mercy is a covering to all who come to you. I cannot
stay on the outside of your love when you rush quickly to
meet me as I approach you.

I will see your goodness as I spend time soaking in your
presence. It is pure life to my thirsty soul. Every lack I find
within myself is filled in the outflow of your mercy. You are
so good! As I gaze upon you, your kindness is exemplified
in my heart.

Great God, you are so abundant in mercy. Let me see more
of your glory than I've ever seen before. Your goodness
surrounds me, of that I'm sure. Give me eyes to see you all
around and encourage my heart to hope as I hide myself in
your love.

Present Peace

May the Lord of peace himself give you peace at all times and in every way. The Lord be with all of you.

2 Thessalonians 3:16 niv

Your peace, God, is no small thing. It is not a consolation prize, and it is not a vain longing. When I have peace, I am dwelling in the stillness of your heart. I don't need to wait until the chaos of my life subsides to experience this perfect peace. You calm every storm, and you can certainly calm the storms of my heart so I experience confident trust.

Today is the perfect opportunity to invite your presence to dwell within me, calming every anxiety and stilling every worry. Your presence is always with me. There are no conditions under which I am outside of your mercy and grace. Where I would keep myself in cycles of shame and chaos, help me to yield my heart instead to your embrace.

God of peace, you are my perfect portion. In every moment your love is available. I submit my heart to you again, giving you full access. Breathe your peace into my soul, calming my busy mind. May I live with your peace actively sustaining and revitalizing my being.

Freed from Fear

I prayed to the LORD, and he answered me.
He freed me from all my fears.
Those who look to him for help
will be radiant with joy.

PSALM 34:4-5 NLT

There is no promise you make that will not be fulfilled, Father. You are faithful. You are present. I can be sure that when I pray and seek you, you will answer. Help me to trust your character. When you answer differently than I expect, I don't want to write off your goodness. Help me to reconsider what it looks like instead.

God, you are full of love, and perfect love pushes out every fear. Where worry and dread have stopped me in my tracks, you are faithful to come and pull me out of the sludge. You free me! Help me to look to you even when the waiting feels long. You have not given up or let go of me. May today be the day I experience the breakthrough of liberty, filling me with joy.

Faithful One, your love never leaves us. Meet me in the middle of the doubts and fears that swirl around my mind. I cannot make the wrong things right, but I know that you can. Free me from all my worries as I look to you. You are the one I depend on. I have no other hope.

Healed by Mercy

I have seen what they have done,
but I will heal them.
I will guide them and comfort them
and those who felt sad for them.
They will all praise me.

ISAIAH 57:18 NCV

When I consider your character, God, I cannot escape your faithfulness. Your goodness is on display for all to see. Who is like you? You fully see every wrong done, every selfish ambition, every evil intent, yet you are not marred by such things. You see everything clearly, and still you choose to act in love.

You heal me not because I deserve it, but because it reflects your good nature. Even in my rebellion, I cannot convince you to stop loving me. You are the God of a thousand chances; there is no limit to your love. You promise to guide and comfort me through this life. How could my response be anything but gratitude? Even if it's not, you do not change your strategy.

Merciful God, thank you for your leadership in my life. I submit my heart again to yours today. Heal me, Lord, of all my sickness. Restore the seeping wounds of my heart. I am yours.

The Merciful Way

"If you had known what this means,
'I desire mercy, and not sacrifice,'
you would not have condemned the guiltless."

MATTHEW 12:7 ESV

God, your requirements are so different than any others. You do not demand perfection, nor do you expect me to drive myself into the ground by working. You are full of mercy, compassion, and kindness. The weak and vulnerable are not degraded in your presence. They are welcomed in and covered by love.

When I consider my intentions in interactions with friends, family, and even strangers, what is the fruit of it? Am I living in order to keep up appearances? When it comes down to it, the only obligation I have is that of love. When I choose to walk in the way of mercy, it will change me. I will reflect your good character.

Merciful One, you are a mystery to the world's ways and systems. You do not require success or perfection in order to be worth anything. My worth is found in you, and it always has been. I want to look like you in love. Fill me with your fiery presence that burns away every bad intention. In your kindness, I have found mercy to give away. Thank you, Lord.

Posture of Waiting

By the help of your God, return;
Observe mercy and justice,
And wait on your God continually.

HOSEA 12:6 NKJV

When life gets hectic and I am caught up in the never-ending demands of family, work, and societal expectations, how do I slow down, God? It is not reasonable that I work myself to the bone for a to-do list that keeps growing. You did not design me for burnout but for partnership with you. I find true rest when I train my soul to wait on you even in the chaos.

When I turn (and return) my heart to you, I am practicing intentional submission to you. As I live with mercy and justice as deep values, I am already aligned with your character. I can't help but be changed by you when I am living connected to your heart.

God, I surrender my heart to yours again. Teach me to wait continually on you as I go about my day. You are the strength of my life. Your love is my resolve. Be my help when I get caught up in the chaos. Bring the peace of your presence as I wait on you.

Abundant Love

Our fathers who were delivered from Egypt
didn't fully understand your wonders,
and they took you for granted.
Over and over you showed them
such tender love and mercy!
Yet they were barely beyond the Red Sea
when they rebelled against you.

PSALM 106:7 TPT

When I take you for granted, God, you do not fail to
show up in love and mercy. You are not easily angered,
and you cannot be convinced to abandon compassion.
Your character is not dependent on mine. You abound in
kindness even in my rebellion.

I don't want to avoid you because I fear you will be
disappointed in my choices. Though others may abandon
me, you will never do it. There is nothing I can do, nothing I
can say, nowhere I can go that I can outrun your incredible
love. You are always ready to receive me with your tender
mercy. You will take the ashes of destruction and make
something beautiful.

Father, you are so full of love and mercy. I bring you my
heart and all I've kept hidden for fear that you would
punish me. I know that you are better than the kindest
person I've known, and I trust your heart. Even as I come
trembling, I offer you everything again.

Beginning and End

"I am the Alpha and the Omega—the Beginning and the End. To all who are thirsty I will give freely from the springs of the water of life."

REVELATION 21:6 NLT

It is difficult to imagine someone without beginning or end. As finite people living in a world with clear inceptions and endings, it is almost too much to comprehend eternity. You God, are the source of all life, and you have given me hope in your everlasting nature. Though I cannot grasp the lengths of your love, I can continually grow in my understanding of it as you give me glimpses throughout my life.

What a wonderful gift I have in your Holy Spirit. He has all wisdom, and he freely gives revelations of your perfect nature. I will not be disappointed when I find that your kindness and comfort really does keep on going. What a wonder that I cannot exhaust your love.

Good God, you are the source of all that is pure and true. As I come to you today, fill me with fresh revelation that enlivens my heart and encourages my soul. You are always flowing, never receding, in compassion. Even if I stopped coming to you, you would never give up on me. You are incomparably wonderful.

Defender and Refuge

I will sing of Your power;
Yes, I will sing aloud of Your mercy in the morning;
For You have been my defense
And refuge in the day of my trouble.

PSALM 59:16 NKJV

God, you are the defender of the weak and a place of safety for the vulnerable. When I feel the frailty of my humanity, your power is made perfect in my weakness. You are the strength I need at every moment. When I cannot go on in my own strength, when my motivation wanes, you will refresh me in the power of your presence.

Sometimes, all I can do is run into your shelter, Most High God. Other times, I am carried into your presence when my legs buckle under the weight of suffering. I was never meant to crawl through life barely surviving. I was created to thrive; you restore and revive me from the inside out. Where I am struggling to keep going, help me to find the rest I need in you. Your mercy never fails.

God, you are my refuge. I hide myself in you as you pour your mercy over my life. I need your presence as much as I ever have. Thank you that I need never face any challenge or situation on my own. You are the strength of my life and the encourager of my weary heart.

Steadfast Love

Be mindful of your mercy, O LORD,
and of your steadfast love,
for they have been from of old.

PSALM 25:6 NRSV

God, your loyal love is not a new concept. It was not a new value when Jesus appeared on the scene. Your unwavering, persistent compassion and mercy have always been consistently present. They make up who you are, and you do not change.

You act in kindness; you always have. Where I have misunderstood your character and wrongly accused your intentions, may I have heavenly perspective to see what has always been true. In humility, I offer you my life, inviting you into every part. I can trust you because you are good. You do not need to be reminded of your character; it is for my benefit. May I stir up faith as I consider your faithfulness.

Lord, you have always been full of lovingkindness. Retrain my eyes to see your goodness where I have felt confusion over your character. I know that you never fail. Where things don't line up, I know that it is because I do not see the bigger picture. I yield my heart to yours again and trust your faithfulness to lead me on.

God With Us

"Look! The virgin will conceive a child!
She will give birth to a son,
and they will call him Immanuel,
which means 'God is with us.'"

MATTHEW 1:23 NLT

God with us: what a wonderful gift from heaven! When you came to earth, Jesus, you set the tone for my new reality. I have not been left on my own or to my own devices. You are present with me. What a glorious miracle! Where I have been discouraged, may I clearly see your nearness.

I have been welcomed into your family, which is wonderfully inclusive. Where I have felt isolated and alone, may I be drawn into your heart through the Holy Spirit. There is no sadness too great that your comfort cannot touch it. Where there is sorrow and loss, you meet me right in the middle of it. I need not dress myself up and pretend that it doesn't exist. Where I am, there you are.

Immanuel, you continually meet me with your presence. Jesus, you are the fulfillment of the promises of the Father. Thank you for your Spirit that loves me to life again and again. I honor you, and I remember today that you are closer than my mother or father. Thank you!

Path of Peace

"Because of God's tender mercy,
the morning light from heaven
is about to break upon us,
to give light to those who sit in darkness
and in the shadow of death,
to guide us to the path of peace."

LUKE 1:78-79 NLT

God, you guide me in tender mercy. Your way is full of peace, kindness, and grace. They are the most powerful forces on earth, though apart from you they tend to sound weak. What a wonder that your wisdom is so different from the wisdom of man. Where in this world power equals force and influence, Jesus demonstrated your power through humility.

As I follow you, you lead me into the way of peace. My heart finds rest in your unfailing love, and this perfect peace cannot be taken away by anyone or anything. It your gift to me, given by and through the Holy Spirit who is faithfully with me. Son of Righteousness, shine your light on me and lead me into stillness.

Holy One, I come to you with all of my messiness today. Shine your light of love on me and lead me into rest. I trust you to guide me to your way of peace because you know the way. I don't rely on my own understanding but on your wisdom which supersedes mine. Your way is better.

Hope of the Helpless

LORD, you know the hopes of the helpless.
Surely you will hear their cries and comfort them.

PSALM 10:17 NLT

God, you are undisturbed by the troubles that surround me even as you meet me in my weakness. You weep with those who weep and you heal the broken; you are never dissuaded from your promises or overcome with defeat. You are the victorious one. Next to you, no one measures up!

You are all-powerful and all-knowing. You are full of mercy to the broken and hurting. You rush to my rescue with the comfort of your presence. You are not slow in keeping your promises. Your timeline takes more than my limited understanding into consideration. You are always on time. Help me to take heart that you see, know, and meet me where I am.

God of my hope, all of my expectations lie in you. You are the giver of good gifts and your presence is the most amazing one. Draw nearer as I cry out to you. Be my comfort and my strength. You're all I have!

Time to Look

Sow for yourselves righteousness;
Reap in mercy;
Break up your fallow ground,
For it is time to seek the LORD,
Till He comes and rains righteousness on you.

HOSEA 10:12 NKJV

There is wisdom to be found in you when I look for it, God. There is understanding awaiting me as I ask for your revelation light to shine in my mind. As I seek you, you draw closer to me. Your ways are marked by unfailing love and unending mercy. Your kindness, who can top? There is no one in the world who is more patient in compassion than you.

Help me not to grow tired of looking to you. You are always near and always ready to help. You faithfully rain your love over me, covering me with your presence that brings life. Now is all I am given; this moment is my opportunity. Help me turn my attention to you more and more.

Lord, I look to you today. You are the keeper of my soul and the hope of my entire life. As I turn my attention to you, come close and speak your words of life. Rain your righteousness over me today.

Not Overwhelmed

The name of the Lord is blessed and lifted high!
For his marvelous miracle of mercy protected me
when I was overwhelmed by my enemies.

PSALM 31:21 TPT

God, your mercy is truly a miracle. Even in my attempts to understand it, do I not need to be reminded over and over again of the limitless levels of it? My mind cannot contain the fullness of the compassion and kindness of your heart. I am carried by your mercy in my triumphs and in my defeat. In weakness, you are my strength. You are the defender of my soul. You will not let me fall beyond your grip.

Let today be the day I give you my trust again. When I am overwhelmed, there you are, right in the middle of it all. You breathe peace into my chaos, calming every storm. There is nothing too messy that you cannot clean up. There is no situation too confusing that your wisdom doesn't set straight. Your ways never fail.

Merciful God, you are the one who holds me steady throughout the seasons of life. There is no situation too difficult for you to handle. I lean into your understanding. Cover me in your mercy and protect me when I am overwhelmed. As always, I depend on you.

In the Valley

Even though I walk through the darkest valley,
I will fear no evil, for you are with me;
your rod and your staff, they comfort me.

PSALM 23:4 NIV

Whatever I face in this world, I do it with your constant companionship, my good God. You are always with me. When I walk through dark valleys of suffering, you are with me even then. I can't escape your presence even if I try. I need not fear what lurks in the shadows with you, my present help and protector, leading me through the valley. Everything is as clear as day to you.

Knowing that I am led by a Good Shepherd, my heart can take rest in the comfort of your guidance. Your wisdom never falters. What a glorious hope I have. When my faith wavers, may my heart be strengthened by the presence of your Holy Spirit who ministers to me.

Good Shepherd, you are the leader of my life. In your love I find the comfort that I need and the joy that I long for. There is no one else like you who is perfect in mercy and a constant giver of peace. You are my portion. Lead me on as I lean on you today.

All Things New

He who sits on the throne said,
"Behold, I am making all things new."
And He said,
"Write, for these words are faithful and true."

REVELATION 21:5 NASB

King of heaven and earth, you are faithful and true.
Abounding in love, never-ending in mercy, you freely give
to all who come to you. What looks like an end to me is an
opportunity for new life in your hands, my masterful Maker.
You never quit, and you are not discouraged.

As I prepare for a new year, help me to consider your
nearness. Merciful God, you never leave me. You are with
me in every season no matter what it looks like. I know that
you are working everything together for my good even
if I don't understand it now. I trust you. You never stop
breathing life into dry bones. You make all things new!

Lord over all, you are always faithful. Thank you for never
leaving me—not even for a moment. Fill me with your
presence today and every day. You are the life in my soul:
my joy, my hope, and the confidence of my heart. Walk
with me as I journey on the path of your love.